AQA GCSE

German

Vocabulary, Grammar and Translation Workbook

Gabriela Hallas and Lisa Probert

Published by Pearson Education Limited, 80 Strand, London, WC2R 0RL.

www.pearsonschoolsandfecolleges.co.uk

Copies of official specifications for all Pearson qualifications may be found on the website: qualifications.pearson.com

AQA material is reproduced by permission of AQA.

Edited by Pearson and Newgen KnowledgeWorks

Designed and typeset by Kamae Design and Newgen KnowledgeWorks

Original illustrations © Pearson Education Limited 2025

Illustrated by Beehive Illustrations (Afua Bediako, Tamara Joubert, Andy Keylock, Daniel Limón, Mauro Marchesi, Andrew Pagram) and Newgen KnowledgeWorks

Cover design by Kamae Design

Cover photo and banner extract © Shutterstock/Hybrid Gfx

Written by Gabriela Hallas and Lisa Probert

The rights of Gabriela Hallas and Lisa Probert to be identified as authors of this work have been asserted by them in accordance with the Copyright, Designs and Patents Act 1988.

Select content created using AI based on Pearson learning materials. To maintain the integrity of content in this product, Pearson has a process to validate output prior to publication.

Printed in the UK by Bell & Bain Ltd, Glasgow

First published 2025

29 28 27 26 25

10 9 8 7 6 5 4 3 2 1

British Library Cataloguing in Publication Data

A catalogue record for this book is available from the British Library

ISBN 978 1 292 757377

Notes from the publisher
Pearson has robust editorial processes, including answer and fact checks, to ensure the accuracy of the content in this publication, and every effort is made to ensure this publication is free of errors. We are, however, only human, and occasionally errors do occur. Pearson is not liable for any misunderstandings that arise as a result of errors in this publication, but it is our priority to ensure that the content is accurate. If you spot an error, please do contact us at resourcescorrections@pearson.com so we can make sure it is corrected.

Inhalt

Basic language

1 Translate these everyday words and phrases into English.

1 ja ....
2 nein ....
3 nicht ....
4 okay ....
5 Ach! ....
6 Hallo! ....
7 Auf Wiedersehen! ....
8 Tschüss! ....
9 Bis bald! ....

2 Fill in the missing subject pronouns.

German	*ich*	....	*er*	....	*es*	....	*wir*	*ihr*	....	*sie*
English	I	you (sg)	he	she	....	one/you/we	....	you (plural)	you (formal, sg and pl)	....

3 Write the German words for the days of the week in the correct order, starting with Monday.

Sonntag Mittwoch Freitag Montag Samstag Donnerstag Dienstag

....

....

4 Draw lines to match up the German seasons with the correct pictures.

1 der Frühling
2 der Sommer
3 der Herbst
4 der Winter

a 

b 

c 

d 

5 Fill in the missing letters in the German months of the year.

1 Jan_ar
2 Fe_ruar
3 M_rz
4 April
5 Ma_
6 Jun_
7 Jul_
8 August
9 September
10 O_tober
11 November
12 De_ember

6 Fill in the missing number words in German.

1 ...., eins, zwei, ..., vier, fünf, ..., sieben, acht, neun

2 ...., ..., dreizehn, vierzehn, fünfzehn, sechzehn, ..., achtzehn, neunzehn

3 ...., zwanzig, ..., vierzig, ..., sechzig, siebzig, achtzig, ...

4 (ein)hundert, ..., eine Million

G

To form **ordinal numbers** in German, add ***-te*** to numbers 1 to 19, and ***-ste*** to numbers 20 and higher.
*der/die/das zwei**te**/vier**te**/fünf**te***
the second/fourth/fifth
*der/die/das zwanzig**ste**/hundert**ste***
the twentieth/hundredth
Exceptions are: *der/die/das **erste*** (*the first*), ***dritte*** (*third*), ***siebte*** (*seventh*).

G

To say the date, use the preposition ***am*** followed by the ordinal number with ***-ten*** on the end for 1st to 19th, and ***-sten*** on the end for 21st to 31st.
***am ersten**/zwei**ten**/**siebten** August*
on the first/second/seventh of August
***am** einundzwanzig**sten** September*
on the twenty-first of September

7 Translate these sentences about festivals and celebrations into German. Use words/phrases from the box to help you. There are more words/phrases than you will need.

Karneval Weihnachten Silvester Heiliger Abend Ostern Eid (al-Fitr) Der erste Weihnachtstag

1 Carnival is on the eleventh of March. ....

2 Eid is on the thirtieth of March. ....

3 Easter is on the twentieth of April. ....

4 Christmas Eve is on the twenty-fourth of December.

....

5 New Year's Eve is on the thirty-first of December.

....

8 Fill in the missing colour words in German.

1 Die Hose ist .... (*blue*) und das Hemd ist .... (*yellow*).

2 Der Rock ist .... (*red*) und die Jacke ist .... (*green*).

3 Der Hund ist .... (*grey*) und .... (*brown*).

4 Die Katze ist .... (*black*) und .... (*white*).

9 Match up the German words for places with their English translations. Write the correct letter.

a Switzerland **b** America **c** England **d** the Baltic Sea **e** state, province
f the European Union (EU) **g** Great Britain **h** USA (United States of America)
i the Rhine **j** the Federal Republic (of Germany) **k** Turkey

1 England ....

2 Amerika ....

3 die Türkei ....

4 die Schweiz ....

5 der Rhein ....

6 die USA (Vereinigte Staaten von Amerika) ....

7 das Bundesland ....

8 die Bundesrepublik (BRD) ....

9 die Europäische Union (EU) ....

10 die Ostsee ....

11 Großbritannien ....

10 Separate the words and write out the German sentences about places. Add capital letters, commas and full stops where needed.

1 kölnundmünchensindindeutschland ....

2 wienistinösterreich ....

3 frankreichitalienspanienundgriechenlandsindineuropa

....

Kulturzone Meine Schule, deine Schule

Using articles and plural nouns

1 Draw lines to match up the German words with their English translations.

1 die Jugendlichen
2 das Kind
3 die Schülerin
4 der Lehrer
5 mein Klassenzimmer
6 meine Hausaufgaben

a my classroom
b my homework
c child
d (female) pupil
e (male) teacher
f young people

2 Circle the noun in each sentence, then translate the nouns into English.

1 Wir haben meistens viele Ferien. ....
2 Der typische Schultag beginnt um acht Uhr. ....
3 Das ist eine Klasse. ....
H 4 Das ist ein Gymnasium. ....
H 5 Das ist das britische Schulsystem. ....
H 6 Das ist die Grundschule. ....

3 Fill in the missing indefinite articles.

1 Er hat .... Hose (*f*).
2 Sie kauft .... Rock (*m*).
3 Wir bekommen .... Tasche (*f*).
4 Ihr kauft .... Jacke (*f*).
5 Sie haben .... Hemd (*nt*).
6 Bekommst du .... T-Shirt (*nt*)?

G

The **indefinite article** is translated as 'a' or 'an'. It changes depending on whether the noun that follows is masculine, feminine or neuter.

Nominative

masculine	feminine	neuter
ein	eine	ein

Accusative

masculine	feminine	neuter
ein**en**	eine	ein

4 Circle the definite article in each sentence. Write if it is masculine (m), feminine (f), neuter (nt) or plural (pl).

1 Der Schultag dauert von 7:30 bis 13:00 Uhr. ....
2 Die Ferien dauern zehn Wochen. ....
3 Die Hausaufgaben dauern zwei bis drei Stunden. ....
4 Hier ist das deutsche Schulsystem. ....
5 Hier ist die Direktorin. ....
6 Sie bekommt das Zeugnis. ....

G

The **definite article** is translated as 'the'. It changes depending on whether the noun that follows is masculine, feminine, neuter or plural.

Nominative

masculine	feminine	neuter	plural
der	die	das	die

Accusative

masculine	feminine	neuter	plural
den	die	das	die

G

Nouns form their **plural** in different ways in German. Here are some of the most common ways.

	what changes	**singular**	**plural**
masculine	adds -*e* adds umlaut and -*e*	der Schuh der Rock	die Schuhe die Röcke
feminine	adds -*n* adds -*en*	die Hose die Uniform	die Hosen die Uniformen
neuter	adds -*e* adds -*en* adds umlaut and -*er*	das Jahr das Hemd das Buch	die Jahre die Hemden die Bücher

5 Write the plural forms of these words.

1 die Jacke ....

2 die Schule ....

3 die Prüfung ....

4 der Text ....

H 5 die Liste ....

H 6 das Angebot ....

F 6 Translate these sentences into English.

Some nouns are made from two words. For example, ***Schulbeginn*** is a compound of *Schule* + *Beginn*. To help translate compound nouns, first separate the noun into its two parts. Sometimes you also need to add some other words in English.

1 Ich beginne meine Prüfungen.

....

....

2 Wann ist der Schulbeginn?

....

3 Wo geht sie einkaufen?

....

4 Alle tragen eine Schuluniform.

....

5 Der Schüler hat gute Noten.

....

H 7 Translate these sentences into German.

1 Normally we buy a jacket.

....

2 The teachers mostly teach five lessons a day.

....

3 The children stay in the classroom.

....

4 I don't like the uniform at all.

....

5 We are comparing the school systems.

....

1 Circle the odd one out.

1 Deutsch Englisch Spanisch Mathe
2 Erdkunde interessant Religion Musik
3 Musik Kunst Theater Mathe
4 Chemie Biologie Sport Physik
5 Sport Nachmittag Religion Französisch
6 Wissenschaften Chemie Stunde Physik

	Montag	Dienstag	Mittwoch	Donnerstag	Freitag
1. Stunde	Mathe	Chemie	Englisch	Deutsch	Physik
2. Stunde	Biologie	Englisch	Mathe	Englisch	Chemie
			Pause		
3. Stunde	Deutsch	Französisch	Geschichte	Kunst	Theater
4. Stunde	Englisch	Kunst	Deutsch	Spanisch	Mathe
5. Stunde	Erdkunde	Informatik	Religion	Musik	Biologie
			Mittagspause		
6. Stunde	Musik	Sport	Physik	Sport	Französisch

2 Translate the underlined time phrases into English.

1 <u>In der Pause</u> spiele ich Tennis. ....
2 <u>Am Nachmittag</u> habe ich Geschichte. ....
3 <u>In der ersten Stunde</u> habe ich Mathe. ....
4 <u>Am Morgen</u> habe ich Englisch. ....
5 <u>In der zweiten Stunde</u> habe ich Kunst. ....
6 <u>Dreimal pro Woche</u> habe ich Deutsch. ....

3 Write the correct present tense form of the verb in brackets.

1 Ich .... meine Prüfung nach der Pause. (*beginnen*)
2 Er .... Französisch. (*lernen*)
3 Sie (*They*) .... gute Noten. (*bekommen*)
4 Mathe .... eine Stunde. (*dauern*)
5 Ihr .... Tennis. (*spielen*)
6 Wir .... Kunst nützlich. (*finden*)

G

The **present tense** of regular verbs is formed by adding endings to the stem. Start with the infinitive and take off the *-en* to get the stem. Then add the endings below:

lernen (*to learn*)
ich lern**e**
du lern**st**
er/sie/es/man lern**t**
wir lern**en**
ihr lern**t**
Sie lern**en**
sie lern**en**

4 Write the correct form of *haben* or *sein* to complete each sentence.

1 Sie (*They*) .... gut in Mathe.
2 Ihr .... um 10 Uhr Englisch.
3 Du .... schwach in Kunst.
4 Ich .... ein Buch.
5 Der Tag .... fantastisch.
H 6 Er .... in der Reihe in der Kantine.

G

Haben and ***sein*** are mostly irregular in the present tense.

	haben (*to have*)	**sein** (*to be*)
ich	habe	bin
du	hast	bist
er/sie/es/man	hat	ist
wir	haben	sind
ihr	habt	seid
Sie	haben	sind
sie	haben	sind

5 Rearrange the words to create correct sentences.

1 habe ich Deutsch In der ersten Stunde

....

2 Ich Mathe, weil leicht mag ist das

....

3 nicht Kunst, weil das ist schwierig mag Ich

....

4 einmal Ich lerne pro Woche Englisch

....

5 Ich gern Geschichte, weil nützlich ist lerne das

....

H 6 mag Sport nicht, anstrengend ist weil Ich das

....

A **time phrase** comes first in a sentence, and then the **verb** comes second. For examples, look at exercise 2. What comes after each underlined time phrase?

G

Some **conjunctions** send the verb to the end of the clause. ***Weil* (because)** is an example of one of these conjunctions. There is always a comma before *weil*.

Ich mag Deutsch, ***weil*** *ich es interessant* ***finde****.*

I like German **because** I **find** it interesting.

F 6 Translate these sentences into German.

1 My favourite subject is German.

....

2 At break I talk to my friends.

....

3 In the afternoon, we begin at 2 p.m.

....

4 I don't like history because it's difficult.

....

5 How do you find biology?

....

H 7 Translate these sentences into English.

1 Ich mag Geschichte lernen.

....

2 Kunst ist mein Lieblingsfach.

....

3 Was hast du am Montag in der ersten Stunde?

....

4 Warum findest du Physik praktisch?

....

5 Am Nachmittag mache ich wissenschaftliche Fächer.

....

2 Was trägst du in der Schule?

Using adjectives with nouns

1 Match the words to the pictures. Write the correct letter.

1 die Schuhe .... B is a pair of shoes
2 das Kleid ....
3 der Rock ....
4 die Hose ....
5 die Jacke ....
6 das Hemd ....

a

b

c
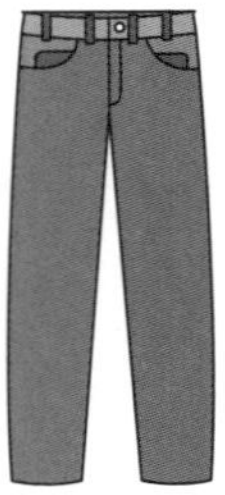
d
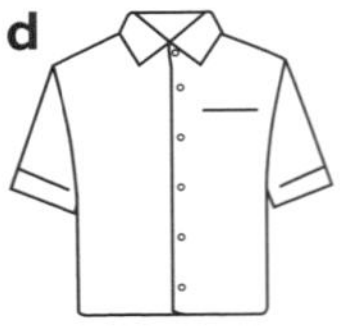
e

f

2 Choose the correct colour(s) from the box to complete each sentence.

1 Das T-Shirt ist .... (*yellow*)
2 Die Schuhe sind .... und .... (*green / white*)
3 Die Hose ist .... (*blue*)
4 Das Hemd ist .... und .... (*red / brown*)
5 Der Rock ist .... (*black*)
6 Die Jacke ist .... (*dark grey*)

rot	gelb
grün	blau
schwarz	weiß
dunkelgrau	braun

3 Fill in the gaps with the correct form of the adjective in brackets.

1 Ich trage eine .... Jacke. (*gelb*)
2 Ich trage einen .... Rock. (*blau*)
3 Wir tragen .... Schuhe. (*schwarz*)
4 Die Jungen im Hintergrund tragen eine .... Hose. (*grau*)
5 Die Mädchen vorne tragen ein .... Hemd, aber kein T-Shirt. (*weiß*)
6 Sie trägt ein .... Kleid. (*hellbraun*)

G

We use **adjectives** to describe things. When we put the adjective before the noun, it has to agree with the gender of the noun and takes the following endings.

Ich trage	ein**en** / kein**en**	blau**en**	Rock.
	eine / keine	blau**e**	Hose
	ein / kein	blau**es**	Kleid.
	–	blau**e**	Schuhe.
	keine	blau**en**	

ein(e)(n) means 'a'/'an'.
kein(e)(n) means 'not a' / 'not any' / 'no' (e.g. I am **not** wearing a blue skirt).

4 Complete the translations into German.

1 Ich trage .... (*brown shoes*).
2 Ich trage .... (*a blue dress*).
3 Er trägt .... (*red trousers*).
4 Sie trägt .... (*a black skirt*).
H 5 Wir tragen .... (*a dark green T-shirt*).
H 6 Sie tragen sowohl .... (*a light grey jacket*) als auch .... (*a grey shirt*).

G

Some verbs, such as ***tragen*** (to wear), add an umlaut in the *du* and *er/sie/es/man* forms.
Some other verbs that follow the same pattern are:
fahren (to drive, go): *ich fahre* → *du fährst*
schlafen (to sleep): *ich schlafe* → *er schläft*

tragen (*to wear*)	
ich	trage
du	tr**ä**gst
er/sie/es/man	tr**ä**gt
wir	tragen
ihr	tragt
Sie	tragen
sie	tragen

5 Fill in the gaps with the correct form of the verb in brackets.

1 Ich .... mit dem Fahrrad zur Schule. (*fahren*)

2 Die Jungen .... eine schwarze Hose. (*tragen*)

3 Das Mädchen .... ein blaues Kleid. (*tragen*)

4 Er .... mit dem Bus. (*fahren*)

5 Wir .... immer gut. (*schlafen*)

H 6 .... ihr Kleidung in Mode? (*tragen*)

F **6 Translate these sentences into English.**

1 Auf dem Foto gibt es vier Jugendliche.

....

2 Im Hintergrund gibt es drei Jungen im Park.

....

3 Sie spielen Fußball und lächeln.

....

4 Das Mädchen vorne lacht.

....

5 Man trägt eine schwarze Hose und ein weißes Hemd.

....

H **7 Translate these sentences into German.**

1 In the background there is a girl.

....

2 She is wearing a yellow dress.

....

3 What colour do you like?

....

4 I speak to my friends in the break.

....

5 The fashion is a blue dress and white shoes.

....

3 Sind Schulregeln wirklich nötig?

Using modal verbs: *müssen, dürfen, sollen* • Using opinion phrases with *dass*

1 Find the places in the school on the plan. Write the correct letter.

1 das Klassenzimmer ....
2 der Gang ....
3 die Kantine ....
H 4 der Computerraum ....
H 5 der Hof ....
H 6 die Turnhalle ....

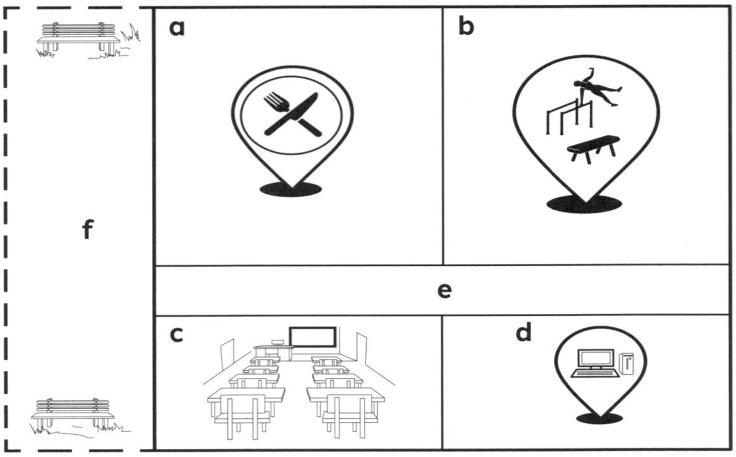

2 Translate these English infinitives into German.

1 to show ....
2 to talk ....
3 to eat ....
4 to drink ....
5 to speak ....
H 6 to disturb ....

3 Complete these sentences with the correct form of the verb in brackets.

1 Man .... die Uniform tragen. (*müssen*)
2 Man .... die Klassenarbeit machen. (*sollen*)
3 Ich .... den Text lesen. (*müssen*)
4 Man .... im Unterricht nicht reden, weil das nicht erlaubt ist. (*dürfen*)
5 Wir .... im Computerraum nicht trinken, weil das verboten ist. (*dürfen*)

G We can use **modal verbs** to talk about what we are allowed to do, what we must do and what we should do.

	dürfen (*to be allowed to, may*)	**müssen** (*to have to, must*)	**sollen** (*to be supposed to, should*)
ich	darf	muss	soll
du	darfst	musst	sollst
er/sie/es/man	darf	muss	soll
wir	dürfen	müssen	sollen

4 Complete the sentences using a verb from the box.

sein	melden	laufen
essen	stören	spielen

1 Man darf im Klassenzimmer nicht ....
You are not allowed to eat in the classroom.

2 Man muss immer pünktlich ....
You must always be punctual.

H 3 Wir sollen drinnen nicht Fußball ....
We should not play football inside.

H 4 Wir dürfen im Hof .... Wieso nicht?
We are allowed to run in the yard. Why not?

H 5 Wir dürfen im Unterricht nicht ....
We mustn't disturb in class.

H 6 Jeden Tag zu Schulbeginn muss man sich ....
Every day at the start of school you have to register.

G When we use modal verbs, the second verb of the sentence is always in the **infinitive form** and goes to the end of the clause or sentence.

5 Write full sentences by linking the two parts with *dass*.

1 Ich glaube / Diese Regel ist sehr wichtig.

....

....

2 Ich denke / Es ist so falsch und langweilig.

....

H 3 Ich finde / Diese Regeln sind nicht notwendig.

....

H 4 Ich denke / Meine Kleidung zeigt meinen Charakter.

....

H 5 Ich glaube / Es ist richtig, weil wir viel lernen müssen.

....

> **G** The **conjunction *dass* (that)** sends the verb to the end of the clause, like *weil* does. There is always a comma before *dass*.

F 6 Translate these sentences into German.

1 I am allowed to speak in class.

....

2 You aren't allowed to eat in the classroom.

....

3 Why do you find it wrong?

....

4 It's very uncomfortable in the canteen.

....

5 I find this rule very right and important.

....

H 7 Translate these sentences into English.

1 Man darf keine Handys im Unterricht benutzen.

....

2 Wir sollen im Gang leise sein.

....

3 Ich finde, dass diese Regel nicht gerecht und total nutzlos ist.

....

4 Ich bin der Meinung, dass ich eigentlich zu viele Hausaufgaben habe.

....

5 Das ist schwer, weil es in der Kantine nicht genug Platz gibt.

....

4 Schultage: die beste Zeit deines Lebens?

Using the perfect and imperfect tenses

1 Translate these compound nouns into English.

1 Sporttag ....

2 Theaterstück ....

3 Klassenfahrt ....

4 Schülerkonzert ....

H 5 Modewoche ....

H 6 Schulausflug ....

Remember to separate compound nouns into their component parts to help with working out the meaning.

2 Write the English translation of the German infinitive. Then draw lines to match each German infinitive with its past participle.

	Infinitive	Past participle
1	schwimmen	gegangen
2	fahren	gegessen
3	essen	gekauft
4	kaufen	geschwommen
5	gehen	gezeigt
6	zeigen	gefahren

3 Circle the correct form of the auxiliary verb to complete each sentence.

1 Ich **bin** / **habe** / **bist** zehn Kilometer zu Fuß gegangen.

2 Er **hat** / **haben** / **ist** im Meer geschwommen.

3 Ich **habe** / **bin** / **habt** die Kleidung gezeigt.

4 Sie **sind** / **haben** / **seid** Pommes gekauft.

5 Ich **habe** / **ist** / **bin** mit dem Fahrrad gefahren.

6 Du **sind** / **seid** / **bist** zu Hause geblieben.

G To form the **perfect tense** you need an **auxiliary verb**. This can be the present tense of *haben* or *sein*. We always use *sein* for verbs of movement like *gehen* (to go) and *schwimmen* (to swim).

4 Fill in the gaps with the past participle of the verb in brackets. Some are irregular.

1 Ich habe ein Konzert .... (*machen*)

4 Du bist einkaufen .... (*gehen*)

3 Er ist mit dem Bus zur Schule .... (*kommen*)

4 Er hat die Hauptrolle .... (*spielen*)

5 Ihr habt etwas .... (*essen*)

6 Wir haben .... (*singen*)

G To form the **past participle** of regular verbs, take off *-en* from the infinitive, and add *ge-* to the front of the stem and *-t* to the end of the stem. For example:
hören ⟶ *gehört*
Some verbs have irregular past participles and you will need to learn these.

G

We use the **imperfect tense** to say what something **was/used to be** like or what someone **had/used to have**.

	sein (*to be*)	**haben** (*to have*)
ich	war	hatte
du	warst	hattest
er/sie/es/man	war	hatte
wir	waren	hatten
ihr	wart	hattet
Sie	waren	hatten
sie	waren	hatten

5 Fill in the gaps with the correct imperfect tense form of *haben* or *sein*.

1 Ich .... so viele Fragen.

2 Die Busfahrt .... 16 Kilometer lang.

3 Ich .... glücklich, weil mein Zeugnis so gut ....

4 Sie (*They*) .... froh, aber auch sehr müde.

H 5 Es ist jetzt vorbei, aber wir .... alle viel Spaß.

H 6 In der Grundschule .... er viele Freunde.

F 6 Translate these sentences into English.

1 Letzte Woche bin ich einkaufen gegangen.

....

2 Am Montag bin ich 16 Kilometer zu Fuß gegangen.

....

3 Letztes Jahr habe ich Musikinstrumente im Konzert gespielt.

....

4 Gestern haben wir kreative Dinge gemacht.

....

5 Wir waren froh, weil das Wetter gut war.

....

H 7 Translate these sentences into German.

1 I showed great clothes.

....

2 I played the main role in a play.

....

3 The teacher swam twenty kilometres.

....

4 We had fun. ....

5 I did lots of creative things because I had no homework.

....

5 Austausch geht auch online!

Using the perfect and imperfect tenses • Speaking and writing in the past and present

1 Fill in the missing English or German translations.

	a minute		a week	a year
eine Sekunde	*eine Minute*	*eine Stunde*		

2 Draw lines to match up the questions and answers.

1 Kannst du deine Schule beschreiben?

2 Was machst du in der Mittagspause?

3 Was hast du gestern nach der Schule gemacht?

4 Was machst du heute nach der Schule?

5 Wie viele Stunden habt ihr pro Tag?

a Ich bin nach Hause gegangen.

b Sie ist ziemlich groß.

c Heute mache ich meine Hausaufgaben.

d Wir haben fünf Stunden und eine Stunde dauert siebenundfünfzig Minuten.

e Meine Freunde und ich verbringen Zeit miteinander.

3 Rewrite the English translations, correcting the error(s).

G You can use the **present tense** to talk about the future, by using future time phrases:
Heute nach der Schule verbringen wir *Zeit miteinander.*
Today after school we're spending time together.

1 Heute nach der Schule mache ich Sport.
Today after school I did sport.

....

....

2 Morgen gehe ich in einen Club. *Tomorrow I went to a club.*

....

3 Heute nach den Stunden esse ich einen Imbiss. *Today after lessons I ate a snack.*

....

4 Heute zu Mittag trinke ich eine Cola. *Today at lunchtime I want to drink a cola.*

....

5 Morgen stehe ich früh auf. *Tomorrow I got up early.*

....

4 Use these phrases to write sentences starting with a time phrase.

G The **verb** is always the **second idea** of the sentence in German. If you start with a time phrase, the **verb** and the *subject* change place:
Ich ***esse****. In der Mittagspause* ***esse*** *ich.*

1 Ich lerne Tennis. (*normalerweise*)

....

2 Wir haben Deutsch. (*im Moment*)

....

3 Ich esse. (*in der Mittagspause*) ....

4 Ich mache meine Hausaufgaben. (*jeden Tag*) ....

5 Die Schule endet. (*um drei Uhr*) ....

H **6** Ich rede mit Freunden. (*gerade nach der Schule*) ....

H 5 Write sentences using the elements given. The time phrase indicates the verb tense you need.

> Look carefully at the time phrase to work out the tense you need to use.
> *Heute **esse ich** Pommes.*
> *Gestern **habe ich** Pommes **gegessen**.*
> *Heute **verbringe ich** Zeit mit Freunden.*
> *Gestern **habe ich** Zeit mit Freunden **verbracht**.*

1 oft / ich / Fußball spielen

....

....

2 normalerweise / er / essen / entweder Pommes oder einen Kuchen

....

3 letzte Woche / viel schlafen / weil / müde / ich

....

4 wir / Sport in der Turnhalle / gestern / machen

....

F 6 Translate these sentences into German.

1 I eat in the canteen.

....

2 The lessons last fifty minutes.

....

3 In the break I am doing my homework.

....

4 My friends and I talk to each other.

....

5 Yesterday after school I went to a club.

....

H 7 Translate these sentences into English.

1 Es gibt ungefähr sechshundert Schüler und Schülerinnen.

....

2 Es gab zu viele Hausaufgaben.

....

3 Wir haben zwei Stunden nach der Mittagspause.

....

4 Eine Schuluniform ist sowohl ein Vorteil als auch ein Nachteil.

....

5 Was ist der Titel von dieser Aufgabe?

....

Glossary

bold = this word will appear in Higher exams only

aber	*but, however*
alle	*everyone, everybody (pl)*
Angebot (nt)	*offer, supply*
anstrengend	*exhausting, strenuous, tiring*
Aufgabe (f)	*task, exercise, assignment, job, duty*
aufstehen	*(to) stand up, get up | standing up, getting up*
Austausch (m)	*exchange, replacement*
Beginn (m)	*beginning, start*
beginnen	*(to) begin, start | beginning, starting*
bekommen	*(to) get, receive | getting, receiving*
beschreiben	*(to) describe | describing*
bin	*(I) am | am being*
Biologie (f)	*biology*
bleiben	*(to) stay, remain | staying, remaining*
britisch	*British*
Buch (nt)	*book*
Chemie (f)	*chemistry*
Club (m)	*club*
darf	*(I) am allowed to, may | (she, he, it, one) is allowed to, may*
darfst	*(you (sing informal)) are allowed to, may*
das	*the (nt)*
dass	*that*
dauern	*(to) last, take (time) | lasting, taking (time)*
denken (an + noun); sich dat. denken	*(to) think (of + noun) | thinking (of + noun); (to) imagine | imagining*

der	*the (m)*
deutsch	*German*
die	*the (f), the (pl)*
dies-(er, e, es)	*this, that (m, f, nt)*
diese	*these, those (pl)*
Direktor (m)	*headteacher, principal, director*
drinnen	*inside, indoors*
dunkel	*dark, gloomy*
dürfen	*(to) be allowed to, may*
eigentlich	*actual, real, actually, really*
ein	*a/an (m, nt)*
eine	*a/an (f)*
einem	*(to) one (indirect obj)*
einen	*one (obj)*
einkaufen	*(to) shop | shopping*
einmal	*once*
englisch	*English*
entweder	*either*
Erdkunde (f)	*geography*
erlauben	*(to) allow, permit | allowing, permitting*
erste (r, s)	*first*
es gab	*there was | were | used to be*
es gibt	*there is | are*
essen	*(to) eat | eating*
etwas	*something, some, a little, somewhat*
Fach (nt)	*subject*
fahren	*(to) go (by transport), drive | going, driving*
falsch	*false, wrong*
fantastisch	*fantastic, super, terrific*
Farbe (f)	*colour*

finden; sich acc. finden	*(to) find | finding, (to) be found | being found, (to) find oneself | finding oneself*
Foto (nt)	*photo, photograph*
Frage (f)	*question, query*
französisch	*French*
froh	*happy, glad*
Gang (m)	*corridor, hallway*
gerade	*straight, just, just now, right now*
gerecht	*just, fair*
Geschichte (f)	*history, story*
(aux) ... geschwommen	*swam | (have, has) swum (pp)*
gestern	*yesterday*
glauben (an acc. + noun)	*(to) believe (in + noun), think | believing (in + noun), thinking*
Grundschule (f)	*primary school*
gut	*good, well*
Gymnasium (nt)	*grammar school*
haben	*(to) have | having*
hast	*(you (sing informal)) have | are having*
hat	*(she, he, it, one) has | is having*
hatte	*(I / she, he, it, one) had | used to have | was having*
hatten	*(we/they/you (formal)) had | used to have | were having*
hattest	*(you (sing informal)) had | used to have | were having*
hattet	*(you (pl informal)) had | used to have | were having*
Haupt(straße)	*main (street)*
Hausaufgaben (pl)	*homework*
hell	*light, bright*
Hemd (nt)	*shirt*
Hintergrund (m)	*background*
Hof (m)	*yard*
Hose (f)	*trousers*
Imbiss (m)	*snack, refreshment, snack bar, take away, diner*
Jacke (f)	*jacket*
Jahr (nt)	*year*
(der) Jugendliche, (ein) Jugendlicher	*(the) young person, adolescent, (a) young person, adolescent (m)*
(die, eine) Jugendliche	*(the, a) young person, adolescent (f)*
Junge (m)	*boy*
kannst	*(you (sing informal)) are able to, can*
Kantine (f)	*canteen, cafeteria*
kaufen	*(to) buy | buying*
kein	*not a, no (m, nt)*
keine	*not a (f), not any, no (f, pl)*
Kilometer (m)	*kilometre*
Kind (nt)	*child*
Klasse (f)	*class*
Klassenarbeit (f)	*school test*
Kleid (nt)	*dress*
Kunst (f)	*art*
langweilig	*boring*
lassen; sich dat. ... lassen	*(to) let, allow | letting, allowing; (to) have sth done | having sth done*
laufen	*(to) run, walk | running, walking*
Lehrer (m)	*teacher (m)*
leicht	*light, easy, simple*
leise	*quiet, soft, quietly*

lernen	*(to) learn, study | learning, studying*
letzt-(er, e, es), letzte	*last (m, f, nt), (pl)*
Lieblings(wort)	*favourite (word)*
Liste (f)	*list*
machen	*(to) do, make | doing, making*
Mädchen (nt)	*girl*
Mathematik/ Mathe (f)	*mathematics/ maths*
mein	*my (m, nt)*
meine	*my (f, pl)*
meistens	*mostly*
melden; sich acc. melden	*(to) report, register | reporting, registering; (to) volunteer, enlist, introduce oneself, get in touch | volunteering, enlisting, introducing oneself, getting in touch*
Minute (f)	*minute*
miteinander	*with each other*
Mittag (m)	*noon, midday*
Mode (f)	*fashion*
Musik (f)	*music*
muss	*(I) have to, must | (she, he, it, one) has to, must*
müssen	*(to) have to, must | having to*
musst	*(you (sing informal)) have to, must*
nach Hause	*(to) home*
Nachmittag (m)	*afternoon*
Nachteil (m)	*disadvantage*
normalerweise	*normally, usually*
Note (f)	*mark, grade, (musical) note*
nötig	*necessary, required*
notwendig	*necessary*
nützlich	*useful*
nutzlos	*useless*
oder	*or*
oft	*often, frequently*
Park (m)	*park*
Pause (f)	*pause, break*
Physik (f)	*physics*
Pommes (frites) (pl)	*chips, fries*
Prüfung (f)	*exam(ination), test*
pünktlich	*punctual, in/on time, prompt*
Regel (f)	*rule*
Reihe (f)	*row, line, queue*
Religion (f)	*religion*
richtig	*right, correct*
Rock (m)	*skirt, rock music*
schlafen	*(to) sleep | sleeping*
Schuh (m)	*shoe*
Schule (f)	*school*
Schüler (m)	*pupil, school student (m)*
Schülerin (f)	*pupil, school student (f)*
schwer	*difficult, hard, heavy*
schwierig	*difficult, hard, tough*
sehr	*very, very much*
sein*; **sich dat ... sein**	*(to) be | being;* ***(to) feel | feeling***
Sekunde (f)	*second*
sind	*(we/they/you (formal)) are | are being*
so	*so, thus, the way, such*
soll	*(I) ought to, am supposed to, should | (she, he, it, one) ought to, is supposed to, should*
sollen	*(to) ought to, be supposed to, should*

sollst	*(you (sing informal)) ought to, are supposed to, should*
sowohl ... als auch	*both ... and*
spanisch	*Spanish*
Spaß (m)	*fun, joke*
spielen	*(to) play / playing*
Sport (m)	*sport, PE*
sprechen	*(to) speak, talk / speaking, talking*
stören	*(to) disturb, bother / disturbing, bothering*
System (nt)	*system*
Tag (m)	*day*
Text (m)	*text*
Theater (nt)	*theatre, drama*
Titel (m)	*title*
total	*total, complete, totally, completely*
tragen	*(to) carry, wear / carrying, wearing*
trinken	*(to) drink / drinking*
T-Shirt (nt)	*T-shirt*
Turnhalle (f)	*gymnasium*
typisch	*typical, typically*
überhaupt	*at all, anyway*
und	*and*
ungefähr	*approximately, about*
Uniform (f)	*uniform*
Unterricht (m)	*lessons, classes, teaching, tuition*
unterrichten	*(to) teach, tutor / teaching, tutoring*
verboten	*forbidden, banned*

verbringen	*(to) spend (time) / spending (time)*
vergleichen (mit)	*(to) compare / comparing*
viel	*a lot*
viele	*a lot, many*
vorbei	*past, over*
vorne, vorn	*at/to the front, ahead*
Vorteil (m)	*advantage, benefit*
wann?	*when?*
war	*(I / she, he, it, one) was / used to be*
waren	*(we/they/you (formal)) were / used to be*
warst	*(you (sing informal)) were / used to be*
wart	*(you (pl informal)) were / used to be*
warum?	*why?*
was?	*what?*
weil	*because*
welch-(er, e, es)?, welche?	*which? (m, f, nt), (pl)*
wichtig	*important*
wie?	*how?*
wieso?	*why?*
Wissenschaft (f)	*science*
wissenschaftlich	*scientific*
wo?	*where?*
Woche (f)	*week*
zeigen	*(to) show, point / showing, pointing*
Zeit (f)	*time*
Zeugnis (nt)	*report*
ziemlich	*quite, fairly, pretty*

Kulturzone Kennst du diese Musiker?

Giving opinions • Using intensifiers and qualifiers

1 Unjumble the letters to rewrite the German intensifiers correctly. Then translate them into English.

1 uz	....	....	
2 rhes	....	....	
3 ebosnreds	....	....	
4 zgna	....	....	
5 lchikriwh	....	....	
6 tihcn	....	....	
7 chzimeil	....	....	
H **8** meetrx	....	....	

2 Translate each word (a–f). Then complete each sentence (1–6) using one of the words (a–f).

a Sänger ....
b Fan ....
c Gruppe ....
d Leben ....
e Lied ....
f Musik ....

G You can use **intensifiers** and **qualifiers** to strengthen or weaken your adjectives. They usually go before the adjective they are qualifying.

1 Ich bin ein großer .... von Namika.
2 Herbert Grönemeyer ist der beste ....
3 Die Ärzte sind eine ....
4 Mozart hat klassische .... geschrieben.
5 Das .... ist sehr traurig.
H **6** Wir lesen Informationen über sein ....

3 Underline the intensifier and circle the adjective(s) in each sentence. Then translate these words into English.

1 Dieses beliebte Instrument ist sehr spannend. ....
2 Seine Stimme ist besonders wunderbar. ....
3 Spanische Tanzmusik ist wirklich schnell. ....
4 Ich finde Konzerte zu langweilig.
....
H **5** Er ist ein ganz komischer Star. ....
H **6** Diese österreichische Band produziert ziemlich verrückte Lieder.
....

G You can give your opinion by:

- using an **opinion verb** such as *mögen*, *lieben* and *hassen*:
  *Ich **mag** klassische Musik (nicht).*
  *Ich **liebe** Musikvideos.*
  *Ich **hasse** Rock.*
- using an **adjective**:
  *Das ist **ruhig**.*
  *Dieses Lied ist **laut**.*
  *Ihre Lieder sind **traurig**.*

You can link the two together with a conjunction like *denn* or *weil*. Remember that *weil* sends the verb to the end but *denn* doesn't.

4 Circle the correct word to complete each English translation.

1 Ich mag Rock, denn er ist besonders interessant. — *I like rock music because it is **particularly / quite** interesting.*

2 Ich liebe diese Band, denn er ist sehr musikalisch. — *I love this band because it is **very / completely** musical.*

3 Dieser Musiker ist wirklich bekannt. — *This musician is **not / really** well-known.*

4 Klassische Musik kann ziemlich laut sein. — *Classical music can be **quite / too** loud.*

5 Sein Ton ist ganz spannend. — *His tone is **very / quite** exciting.*

H 6 Alles Andere ist nicht lustig. — *Everything else is not **boring / funny**.*

H 5 Correct the mistakes in each English translation.

1 Diese Band singt sehr wunderbare Lieder. — *This band sings quite loud songs.*

....

2 Sein total berühmtes Lied ist ein Liebeslied. — *His totally famous song is a slow song.*

....

3 Ihr Ton ist wirklich ruhig. — *Her tone is really boring.*

....

5 Ich folge vielen ganz berühmten Stars. — *I follow a lot of not very funny rappers.*

....

6 Letztes Jahr war er extrem unbekannt. — *Last year he was extremely popular.*

....

H 6 Ich finde alles sehr langsam. — *I find everything very bad.*

....

F 6 Translate these sentences into German.

1 I like rock music. ....

2 I love his voice because it's completely relaxing.

....

3 This music is particularly loud. ....

4 This singer is German. ....

5 I didn't listen to this video. ....

H 7 Translate these sentences into English on a separate sheet.

1 Meine Lieblingssängerin ist Namika, weil ihre Musik ziemlich spannend ist.

2 Er stammt aus Deutschland, aber seine Familie ist aus der Türkei.

3 Sie ist wirklich erfolgreich und überall bekannt.

4 Die Musik klingt weder laut noch leise, also mag ich sie.

5 Letzten Monat bin ich auf ein Konzert gegangen und der Sänger hat auf Türkisch gesungen.

Use the glossary at the end of the module to look up any unfamiliar words, and try to learn them.

1 Was machst du gern in deiner Freizeit?

Using frequency phrases with correct word order

1 Translate the German infinitives into English.

1 fernsehen ....

2 hassen ....

3 sich interessieren ....

4 kochen ....

5 lesen ....

6 tanzen ....

7 singen ....

8 hören ....

9 spielen ....

H 10 malen ....

H 11 sich amüsieren ....

H 12 sich treffen ....

2 Underline the frequency expressions, then translate them into English.

1 Am Wochenende koche ich. ....

2 Ich tanze täglich. ....

3 Ab und zu gehe ich Fahrradfahren. ....

4 Ich schwimme manchmal. ....

5 Jeden Tag gehe ich wandern. ....

H 6 Ich zeichne häufig Bilder. ....

G

We can talk about how often we do things using **frequency expressions**. Here are some examples:

jeden Tag/täglich	every day
immer	always
(sehr) oft	(very) often
am Wochenende	at the weekend
jede Woche	every week
manchmal	sometimes
ab und zu	from time to time
selten	seldom
(fast) nie	almost never
H *häufig*	frequently, often

Remember that when you use a frequency expression at the start of the sentence, the verb must stay in second position.

3 Rewrite each sentence using the frequency expression in brackets.

1 Ich gehe ins Kino. (*manchmal*) ....

2 Ich treffe Freunde. (*am Wochenende*) ....

3 Ich lese die Zeitung. (*fast nie*) ....

4 Ich koche zu Hause. (*oft*) ....

5 Meine Freundinnen simsen. (*immer*) ....

6 Ich spiele Tennis in der Stadt. (*ab und zu*) ....

4 Read the grammar boxes on the next page. Then draw lines to match up the questions and the answers. Add an emoticon (💔, ❤ or ❤❤) next to each answer to show how much they like it.

1 Fährst du gern Fahrrad?

2 Gehst du lieber einkaufen oder schwimmen?

3 Was liebst du?

4 Was machst du gern am Computer?

5 Was machst du nicht gern?

6 Was liest du gern?

H 7 Malst du gern?

a Ich mache nicht gern Sport. ....

b Ich gehe lieber einkaufen. ....

c Am Computer sehe ich gern Filme. ....

d Ich fahre nicht gern Fahrrad. ....

e Ich male nicht gern. ....

f Ich bin ein Leser von Romanen. ....

g Ich liebe schwimmen gehen, weil das Spaß macht. ....

G

We use the **present tense** to talk about what we do regularly, or what we are doing.

regular verbs: **singen** (*to sing*)	**verbs with changes to their vowel sounds in the *du* and *er/sie/es/man* forms:** **treffen** (*to meet*)
ich sing**e**	ich treff**e**
du sing**st**	du tr**iffst**
er/sie/es/man sing**t**	er/sie/es/man tr**ifft**
wir sing**en**	wir treff**en**
ihr sing**t**	ihr treff**t**
Sie sing**en**	Sie treff**en**
sie sing**en**	sie treff**en**

G

You can express preferences by using the adverbs ***gern*** or ***lieber*** to qualify verbs:

*Ich singe **gern**.* I **like** singing.

*Ich lese nicht **gern**.* I don't **like** reading.

*Ich spiele gar nicht **gern** Basketball.* I really **dislike** playing basketball.

*Ich treffe sehr **gern** Freunde.* I really **like** meeting friends.

*Ich tanze **lieber**.* I **prefer** dancing.

H **5 Rewrite each sentence. Conjugate the verb in brackets and put the words into the correct order.**

1 ich / einkaufen / jedes Wochenende / (gehen) / im Stadtzentrum ....

2 (zeichnen) / er / schöne / Bilder / liebsten / am ....

3 oft / (machen) / gern / wir / Fotos ....

4 am Computer / (spielen) / gar nicht / ihr / gern ....

5 (besuchen) / deine Freunde / gern / du ....

6 sie (*she*) / Filme / gern / im Kino / (sehen) ....

F **6 Translate these sentences into English.**

1 Ich spiele oft Fußball. ....

2 In meiner Freizeit spiele ich Basketball. ....

3 Liest du lieber Literatur oder Texte? ....

4 Sie fährt täglich Fahrrad. ....

5 Ich treffe gern meine Freunde, denn das ist lustig. ....

H **7 Translate these sentences into German.**

1 I like painting most of all and I draw every day.

....

2 I dance in a club now and again. ....

3 I like music but I prefer doing sport. ....

4 I rarely go hiking because I find it very boring.

....

5 I love reading but I don't like reading novels or the newspaper at all.

....

2 Was machst du online?

Using separable verbs in the present tense

1 Write the words from the cloud in the correct column and write the English translations next to them.

benutzen Bild schauen Ding
Handy Nummer schicken Spieler
digital H Daten H gucken

Nachricht (f) has two meanings: 'news' or 'message'.
There are several ways to say that you are texting:
Ich schicke eine SMS. / eine Nachricht. / eine SMS-Nachricht.
Ich simse.

Nouns	Adjectives	Verbs

2 Complete each sentence using a word from the box.

Kamera Computer SMS-Nachrichten Videos Handy sozialen Medien

1 Ich schaue oft Nachrichten auf ....
2 Mit der .... mache ich schöne Fotos.
3 Ich schreibe nie ....
4 Mit meinem .... rufe ich immer meine Freunde an.
5 Ich streame oft Musik auf dem ....
6 Ich sehe gern lustige .... von Katzen und Hunden.

3 Underline the two parts of the separable verbs in each sentence.

1 Ich lade Fotos hoch.
2 Rufst du deine Freunde an?
3 Er lädt E-Mails herunter.
H 4 Schaut ihr Videos an?
H 5 Ich lade mein Laptop auf.
H 6 Er nimmt Filme auf.

G

Separable verbs contain a separable prefix. In the present tense, this prefix 'snaps off' and goes to the end of the clause.

anrufen (to call, phone)	*Ich* ***rufe*** *meine Freunde* ***an***.
herunterladen (to download)	*Ich* ***lade*** *Fotos* ***herunter***.
ansehen (to watch)	*Ich* ***sehe*** *Filme* ***an***.
H *aufmachen* (to open)	*Ich* ***mache*** *die Tür* ***auf***.
H *annehmen* (to accept, assume)	*Er* ***nimmt*** *das Angebot* ***an***.

4 Rewrite each sentence, putting the words into the correct order.

> Start your sentence with the subject pronoun, which has a capital letter.

1 ruft oft seine an Freunde Er ....

2 Sie geht aus nicht gern ....

3 Bilder herunter Wir laden ....

H 4 Serien schaut Ihr an ....

H 5 holt ihre Schwester ab Sie ....

H 6 alte Handys abgeben und andere Technologie Man kann hier ....

....

H 5 Translate each sentence into German using a verb from the box.

aufnehmen	ansehen	anrufen	herunterladen	aufladen	hochladen

1 How often do you watch soap operas? ....

2 I call my friend. ....

3 They download photos. ....

4 We upload messages. ....

5 You normally record videos. ....

6 She charges her phone. ....

F 6 Translate these sentences into German.

1 I stream music. ....

2 She doesn't like using her computer. ....

3 We send SMSs every day. ....

4 Which apps do you download? ....

5 You never watch television. ....

H 7 Translate these sentences into English.

1 Ich habe viele Geräte, aber mein Lieblingsgerät ist mein Handy.

....

2 Wir können eigentlich alles mit einem Laptop machen.

....

3 Ich bin oft im Netz und habe viele Kontakte in sozialen Medien.

....

4 Wenn ich Zeit habe, lese ich die Nachrichten im Internet.

....

5 Die Technik ist ein positives Ding in meinem Leben.

....

3 Das Leben als Star

Asking questions

1 Draw lines to match up the German words with their English translations.

1 Leistung	**a** job, profession
2 Nachteil	**b** disadvantage
3 Erfolg	**c** bullying
4 Beruf	**d** achievement
5 Mobbing	**e** advantage
6 Vorteil	**f** success
7 Spiel	**g** club, association
8 Verein	**h** game, match

2 Complete each sentence using a word from the box.

Ausstellung Spieler Gegner Tätigkeit Fan Autorin

Use the glossary to look up any words that are unfamiliar and try to learn them.

1 Er spielt Fußball. Er ist ein ....

2 Sie schreibt Bücher. Sie ist eine ....

3 Er folgt Fußballmannschaften. Er ist ein ....

H **4** Er spielt gegen ihn. Er ist sein ....

H **5** Sie arbeitet als Schauspielerin. Das ist ihre ....

H **6** Wir sehen Bilder im Museum. Das ist eine ....

G

To ask yes/no questions, start with the verb followed by the subject pronoun:
Hast du *Haustiere?* **Do you have** pets?
Möchtest du *spielen?* **Would you like** to play?
Willst du *tanzen?* **Do you want** to dance?

3 Write questions by putting the words into the correct order.

1 reisen / möchtest / um die Welt / du ....

2 du / lesen / willst / Buch / ein ....

3 möchtet / fragen / Eltern / eure / ihr ....

4 Mobbing / Problem / ist / ein ....

5 möchten / Spieler / treffen / den / Sie ....

H **6** du / Vorbild / hast / ein ....

4 Complete each question using the correct question word or phrase.

1 .... ist deine Lieblingspersönlichkeit?
Who is your favourite personality?

G

You can also ask questions using **question words**:

Was? What?	*Warum?* Why?
Wo? Where?	*Welch-?* Which?
Wie? How?	*Wann?* When?
Wie viel? How much?, How many?	*Um wie viel Uhr?* At what time?
Wer? Who?	*Wie lange?* How long?
	H *Wieso?* Why?

2 .... endet das Spiel? *At what time does the match end?*

3 .... kann er gut machen? *What can he do well?*

4 .... ist sie berühmt? *Why is she famous?*

5 .... will er fahren? *How does he want to travel?*

H 6 .... ist diese Übung schwierig? *Why is this exercise difficult?*

H 7 .... kann ich dir danken? *How can I thank you?*

H 8 .... stellt sie in ihren Filmen dar? *What does she portray in her films?*

H 5 Write a question for each of these answers.

1 Ich finde Fußball toll. ....

2 Es kommt darauf an, ob ich viele Hausaufgaben habe. ....

3 Ich spiele um Viertel nach drei. ....

4 Das ist eine berühmte Schauspielerin. ....

5 Ich glaube, dass meine Mannschaft gewonnen hat. ....

6 Die Band tritt morgen auf. ....

> ***auftreten*** *to appear, occur, perform*
> ***es kommt darauf an, ob ...*** *it depends whether/if ...*

F 6 Translate these sentences into English.

1 Ich liebe mein Leben. ....

2 Was ist ihr Beruf? ....

3 Mobbing ist ein großes Problem online. ....

4 Ich möchte um die Welt reisen. ....

5 Er hat ein gutes Spiel gehabt. ....

H 7 Translate these sentences into German.

1 I want to see a football match tomorrow evening.

....

> You will need to include 'the' before the name of the football club. (*S.V. stands for Sport-Verein.*)

2 His team is playing at eight o'clock and their opponent is Hamburger S.V.

....

3 Would you prefer to watch a play?

....

4 My role model is an actor and I like him because he fights against bullying.

....

5 My favourite personality is a singer and I saw him last year.

....

4 Wie war der Film?

Using the imperfect and perfect tenses together

1 These adjectives are written in reverse order: write them out correctly. Then translate them into English.

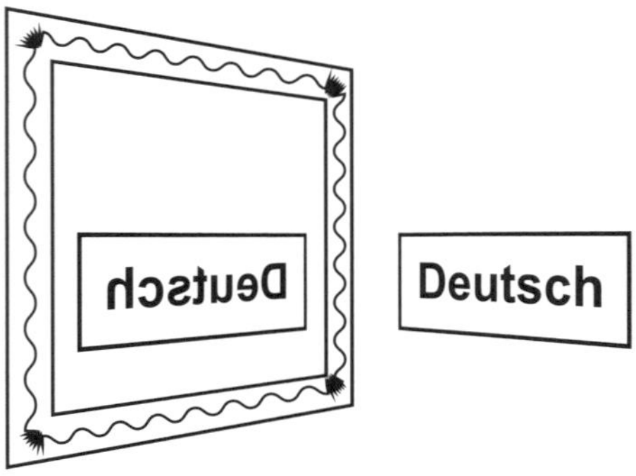

1 hcsimok ....
2 treizilpmok ....
3 gnal ....
4 masgnal ....
5 gitsul ....
6 giruart ....
7 giztiw ....
8 rabrednuw ....

Try to learn as wide a variety of adjectives as possible. You can use intensifiers to strengthen or weaken your adjectives.

total totally	*wirklich* really	*ganz* quite	*fast* almost
extrem extremely	*besonders* particularly	*ziemlich* quite	*nicht* not
sehr very		*ein bisschen* a little	

2 Complete these sentences by translating the word(s) in brackets into German.

You can use ***denn*** or ***weil*** to say 'because'. Remember that *weil* sends the verb to the end of the sentence, but *denn* does not.

1 Ich finde diese .... (*comedy*) .... (*totally*) modern.
2 Ich mag diesen .... (*film*), weil er .... (*quite*) perfekt ist.
3 Auf diesem .... (*channel*) gibt es .... (*very*) gute Sendungen.
4 In dieser .... (*soap opera*) gibt es .... (*too*) viel Gewalt und die Schauspieler rufen .... (*almost*) immer.
5 Die .... (*viewers*) sehen gern Krimis, denn sie sind .... (*quite*) spannend.
6 Das .... (*audience*) sieht nicht gern langsame Filme, weil sie .... (*a little*) langweilig sind.

3 Complete these perfect tense sentences with the past participle of the verb in brackets.

1 Ich bin diesmal ins Kino .... (*gehen*)
2 Ich habe eine Seifenoper .... (*sehen*)
3 Ich habe einen Krimi .... (*schauen*)
4 Ich habe die Sendung zu kompliziert .... (*finden*)
5 Ich habe eine Komödie .... (*schreiben*)
6 Ich habe eine Kritik .... (*lesen*)

G

To say what happened or what has happened, we use the **perfect tense**:
*Ich **habe** den Film **gesehen**.* I **saw** / I **have seen** the film.
*Ich **habe** die Serie toll **gefunden**.* I **found** / I **have found** the series great.
We can also use the **imperfect tense** when we're talking about past events:

ich war I was	*ich hatte* I had
es war it was	*es hatte* it had

4 Complete these sentences with an imperfect tense verb from the box.

waren	fand	warst	gab	hatte	war

1 Der Film .... wunderbar.

2 Die Schauspieler .... toll.

3 Ich .... viel Spaß.

H 4 Es .... viele Filme.

H 5 Ich .... die Serie super.

H 6 .... du zu Hause?

G

The **perfect tense** is used in spoken German and more informal writing:

ich habe gesungen I have sung / I sang

ich habe gefunden I have found / I found

The **imperfect tense** is used more in written narrative accounts, stories and reviews:

H *ich sang* I sang

H *ich fand* I found

H 5 Rewrite each sentence, replacing the underlined verb with the correct form of the perfect (P) or imperfect (I) tense as indicated in brackets.

1 Die Werbungen <u>sind</u> sehr laut. (I)

....

2 Er <u>schreibt</u> eine Kritik über die letzte Szene. (P)

....

3 Es <u>gibt</u> vier Folgen und der Schluss <u>ist</u> total spannend. (I)

....

4 Wir <u>sehen</u> einen interessanten Film über die Geburt und den Tod von einem Hund. (P)

....

5 Diese Sendung handelt von Komödien. Ich <u>finde</u> den Inhalt lustig. (I)

....

6 Es tut mir leid, aber du <u>kommst</u> zu spät. (P)

....

F 6 Translate these sentences into German.

1 I find comedies totally funny. ....

2 I like detective stories because they are interesting.

....

3 I watch a soap opera on this channel. ....

4 I found the film perfect. ....

5 The viewers were sad. ....

H 7 Translate these sentences into English on a separate sheet.

1 Es gibt etwa sechs volle Serien und das ist super.

2 Krimis erschrecken das Publikum.

3 Es dreht sich um den Himmel und die Erde.

4 Es gab viel Spannung und Stimmung im Film.

5 Ich will den Rest sehen, weil die Sendungen wichtige Informationen berichten.

Don't be disheartened if you don't know some of these words yet! Use the glossary at the end of the module to help you.

5 Hast du Pläne?

- Using the future tense to describe plans for the weekend
- Using the 'time – manner – place' rule

1 Translate the sequencers using the English words in the box.

at last	afterwards	first (of all)	then	eventually	after

1 zuerst .... **3** danach .... **5** endlich ....

2 dann .... **4** nachdem .... **6** schließlich ....

2 Draw lines to match up the sentence halves.

1 Ich werde mit Freunden eine Party
2 Er wird mit seinem Freund zum Strand
3 Wir werden zu Hause Bücher
4 Sie wird mit ihrer Freundin Videos
5 Ich werde vielleicht mit der Familie Fußball
6 Wirst du Rock im Park

a streamen.
b machen.
c lesen.
d hören?
e gehen.
f spielen.

3 Circle the correct part of *werden* to complete these sentences.

1 Ich **wird** / **werde** / **werden** Fußball spielen.
2 **Werde** / **Wirst** / **Werden** du allein Sport machen?
3 Er **werden** / **werde** / **wird** mit seinem Freund Musik üben.
4 Wir **wird** / **werde** / **werden** mit der Familie einen Film sehen.
5 Ich **wird** / **werde** / **werden** mein Handy benutzen.
6 Welche Aktivität **wirst** / **werden** / **wird** du machen?

G

We use the **future tense** to say what we **will** do. To form this, use the present tense of ***werden*** and put the infinitive of another verb at the end of the clause.

*Ich **werde** einen Film im Kino sehen.* I **will** see a film in the cinema.
***Wirst** du in der Stadt einkaufen gehen?* **Will** you go shopping in town?
*Er **wird** fernsehen.* He **will** watch TV.
*Wir **werden** im Fitness-Studio tanzen.* We **will** dance in the gym.

4 Put the words into the correct order to make sentences. Remember the 'time – manner – place' rule.

The correct word order for elements in a German sentence is:
1 time, **2 manner**, **3 place**.
So we need to say: **1 when** we're doing the activity, **2 how** we're doing the activity, and **3 where** we're doing the activity.

1 Ich später allein an den Strand gehen werde

....

2 heute Abend Er mit Familie der wird Videos streamen

....

3 werden mit Freunden im Park spielen Wir Tennis Nachmittag heute

....

4 mit Freundin meiner Ich morgen früh werde im Kino sehen Film einen

....

5 allein wird heute Sie Nacht Hause Bücher zu lesen

....

H **6** am Morgen mit der werden der einkaufen Wir Familie in Stadt gehen

....

H 5 Complete the German translations.

1 *Afterwards, I will go shopping with my friends.*

Danach .... ich mit meinen .... einkaufen ....

2 *Finally he will spend a lot of money.*

Schließlich .... er ....

3 *At the weekend she will do everything else in town with friends.*

Sie .... alles Andere mit Freundinnen in der Stadt ....

4 *He will watch a film about heaven and Earth.*

Er .... einen Film über den Himmel und die Erde ....

5 *At the weekend we will play tennis in the park with friends.*

Am Wochenende .... wir .... Tennis ....

6 *We will stream videos earlier at 3:30 with the family.*

Wir .... eher um halb vier .... Videos ....

F 6 Translate these sentences into English.

1 Am Wochenende gehe ich schwimmen.

....

2 Ich werde am Sonntag allein zu Hause Videos streamen.

....

3 Er ist mit seinem Freund zum Strand gegangen

....

4 Wir werden später mit der Familie im Fernsehen einen Film sehen.

....

5 Das wird toll sein. ....

H 7 Translate these sentences into German.

1 This afternoon I'm buying a ticket because my favourite band is performing next week.

....

2 Afterwards I will go shopping in town with my friends.

....

3 That will be totally wonderful because I really like going to the theatre.

....

4 I went to the cinema with my friend and we watched a film.

....

5 What will you do next weekend? ....

Glossary

bold = this word will appear in Higher exams only

ab und zu	*now and again, (every) now and then*
Abend (m)	*evening*
abgeben	*(to) give in, hand in, submit*
abholen	*(to) get, fetch, pick up*
Aktivität (f)	*activity*
allein, alleine	*alone*
alles	*everything (sing.), all*
alles (Andere)	*everything (else)*
also	*so, therefore*
am liebsten	*(the) most preferred (post-noun), most preferably, rather*
amüsieren; sich acc. amüsieren	*(to) enjoy (oneself), to have a good time*
annehmen	*(to) accept, assume*
anrufen	*(to) ring, phone | ringing, phoning*
anschauen	*(to) look at, watch*
ansehen; sich dat. ansehen	*(to) look at, watch | looking at, watching*
App (f) (nt)	*app*
aufladen	*(to) charge | charging*
aufmachen	*(to) open | opening*
aufnehmen	*(to) take in, record*
auftreten	*(to) appear, occur, perform*
ausgehen	*(to) go out | going out*
Ausstellung (f)	*exhibition, show*
Autor (m)	*author, writer*
Band (f)	*band, group (music)*
Basketball (m)	*basketball*
bekannt	*well-known, famous*
benutzen	*(to) use | using*
berichten	*(to) report | reporting*
berühmt	*famous*
besonders	*particularly, especially*
Bild (nt)	*picture, image, photo*
(ein) bisschen	*a little*
Computer (m)	*computer*
danken	*(to) thank | thanking*
dann	*then*
darstellen	*(to) depict, portray, show, represent*
Daten (pl)	*data*
denn	*because*
diesmal	*this time*
digital	*digital, digitally*
Ding (nt)	*thing, object*
drehen; sich drehen um + noun	*(to) film, turn, (to) be about + noun*
eher	*earlier, sooner, rather*
E-Mail (f) (nt)	*e-mail*
enden	*(to) end, finish | ending, finishing*
endlich	*finally, at last, eventually*
erschrecken	*(to) frighten, be startled*
es kommt darauf an, ob ...	*it depends*
es tut mir leid	*I'm sorry*
etwa	*about, approximately*
Fan (m)	*fan, supporter*
fand	*(I, she, he, it) found*

German	English	😐	🙂	😎
fast	*almost, nearly*			
fernsehen	*(to) watch television | watching television*			
Fernsehen (nt)	*television*			
Film (m)	*film, movie*			
Folge (f)	*result, consequence, episode (TV)*			
folgen	*(to) follow | following*			
fragen (nach + noun); sich fragen	*(to) ask (about + noun) | asking; (to) wonder | wondering*			
Freizeit (f)	*spare time, free time, leisure time*			
früh	*early*			
Fußball (m)	*football, soccer*			
ganz	*whole, all the, quite*			
gar	*at all*			
Geburt (f)	*birth*			
Gegner (m)	*opponent, competitor, enemy, rival*			
gehen (in + noun); gehen um + noun	*(to) go (to + noun) | going; to be about + noun | being about*			
Gerät (nt)	*tool, piece of equipment, appliance*			
gern, gerne	*gladly, (with a verb) like to*			
Gewalt (f)	*violence, force*			
Gruppe (f)	*group, band*			
gucken, kucken	*(to) look, watch*			
halb	*half*			
handeln; sich handeln um + noun	*(to) deal, trade; to be about + noun*			
Handy (nt)	*mobile phone*			
hassen	*(to) hate, detest | hating, detesting*			

German	English	😐	🙂	😎
häufig	*frequent, frequently, often*			
herunterladen	*(to) download | downloading*			
Himmel (m)	*sky, heaven*			
hochladen	*(to) upload | uploading*			
hören, hören auf acc. …	*(to) hear, listen | hearing, listening, (to) obey someone | obeying someone*			
immer	*always*			
Inhalt (m)	*content, plot*			
Instrument (nt)	*instrument*			
interessant	*interesting*			
interessieren; sich acc. interessieren (für + noun)	*(to) interest | interesting; (to) be interested (in + noun) | being interested*			
jed-(er, e, es)	*each, every (m, f, nt)*			
Kamera (f)	*camera*			
kann	*(I) am able to, can / (she, he, it, one) is able to, can*			
Karte (f)	*card, ticket, menu*			
Kino (nt)	*cinema, movies, pictures*			
klassisch	*classical*			
klingen	*(to) sound, ring*			
kochen	*(to) cook, boil | cooking, boiling*			
komisch	*funny, comical, strange, odd, weird*			
Komödie (f)	*comedy*			
kompliziert	*complicated, complex*			
können	*(to) be able to, can | being able to*			
Kontakt (m)	*contact*			
Konzert (nt)	*concert*			

Module 2: Glossary

Krimi (m)	*thriller, detective story/film, crime story/film*
Kritik (f)	*criticism, review*
lang	*long*
langsam	*slow, slowly*
Laptop (m) (nt)	*laptop*
lesen	*(to) read | reading*
Leser (m)	*reader*
Liebe (f)	*love*
lieben	*(to) love | loving*
lieber	*more gladly, rather*
Lied (nt)	*song*
Literatur (f)	*literature*
lustig	*funny, enjoyable*
malen	*(to) paint | painting*
manchmal	*sometimes*
Medien (pl)	*media*
Mobbing (nt)	*bullying*
möchte	*(I, she, he, it, one) would like (to)*
möchten	*(we/they/you (formal)) would like (to)*
möchtest	*(you (sing informal)) would like (to)*
möchtet	*(you (pl informal)) would like (to)*
modern	*modern, up-to-date*
mögen	*(to) like | liking*
morgen	*tomorrow*
Morgen (m)	*morning*
musikalisch	*musical*
Nachricht (f)	*news, message*
nächst-(er, e, es), nächste	*next (m, f, nt), (pl)*
Nacht (f)	*night*
Netz (nt)	*net, network, web*
nie	*never*
Nummer (f)	*number*
online	*online*
österreichisch	*Austrian*
Party (f)	*party*
perfekt	*perfect, perfectly*
produzieren	*(to) produce | producing*
Programm (nt)	*program (IT), channel (TV)*
Publikum (nt)	*audience, public*
reisen	*(to) travel | travelling*
Rest (m)	*rest, remainder*
Roman (m)	*novel*
rufen	*(to) call, shout*
Sänger (m)	*singer*
schauen	*(to) look | looking*
Schauspieler (m)	*actor*
schicken	*(to) send | sending*
schließlich	*finally, eventually*
Schluss (m)	*end, conclusion, finish, closure*
schnell	*quickly, fast*
schreiben (an acc. + noun)	*(to) write (to + noun) | writing*
sehen	*(to) see, watch | seeing, watching*
Seifenoper (f)	*soap opera, series*
selten	*rare, rarely*
Sendung (f)	*programme*
Serie (f)	*series*
simsen	*(to) text | texting*
singen	*(to) sing | singing*
SMS (f)	*text message*
soziale Medien (pl)	*social media*
spannend	*exciting, thrilling*
Spannung (f)	*suspense, tension*
spät	*late*
Spiel (nt)	*game, match*

Spieler (m)	*player*
stammen aus + noun	*(to) come from + noun*
Star (m)	*celebrity, headliner*
Stimme (f)	*voice, vote*
Stimmung (f)	*mood, atmosphere*
streamen	*(to) stream / streaming*
Stück (nt)	*piece, play (theatre)*
super	*super*
Szene (f)	*scene*
täglich	*daily, every day*
tanzen	*(to) dance / dancing*
Tätigkeit (f)	*activity, work, occupation*
Technik (f)	*technology, technique*
Technologie (f)	*technology*
Tennis (nt)	*tennis*
Tod (m)	*death*
toll	*great, amazing*
Ton (m)	*sound, tone*
traurig	*sad*
treffen; sich acc. treffen	*(to) meet / meeting; (to) meet up, get together / meeting up, getting together*
türkisch	*Turkish*
üben	*(to) practise / practising*
überall	*everywhere*
Übung (f)	*exercise, practice*
Uhr (f)	*clock, watch, o'clock*
Verein (m)	*association, club, society*
verrückt	*crazy, insane, mad*
Video (nt)	*video*
vielleicht	*perhaps, maybe, possibly*
Viertel (nt)	*quarter*
voll	*full, complete*
wandern	*(to) (go on a) walk or hike, ramble / (going on a) walk or hike, rambling*
Werbung (f)	*advertising, advert(isement)*
werden	*(to) become / becoming / (we/they/you (formal)) become / are becoming / will (aux)*
will	*(I) want (to) / (she, he, it, one) wants (to)*
willst	*(you (sing informal)) want (to)*
wird	*(she, he, it, one) becomes / is becoming / will (aux)*
wirklich	*real, actual, really, actually, truly*
wirst	*(you (sing informal)) become / are becoming / will (aux)*
witzig	*funny, witty, comical*
Wochenende (nt)	*weekend*
wollen	*(to) want (to) / wanting (to)*
wunderbar	*wonderful*
zeichnen	*(to) draw / drawing*
Zeitung (f)	*newspaper*
Zuschauer (m)	*viewer, spectator*

Foundation translation revision

German to English

1 Colour one box from each column to translate each sentence (1–4) into English. Use a different colour for each sentence. Then write out your translations.

I	is	biology	interesting.
I	we get	very	music.
This book	like	the	easy.
Every week	find	classical	grades.

1 Ich mag klassische Musik. ....

2 Dieses Buch ist sehr interessant. ....

3 Jede Woche bekommen wir die Noten. ....

4 Ich finde Biologie einfach. ....

2 Underline the mistake(s) in the English translations. Then write out the correct English translations.

1 Ich mag diese Sendung. — *I like this film.*

....

2 Diese Seifenoper ist wunderbar, denn die Schauspieler sind toll. — *This programme is wonderful because the actors are bad.*

....

3 Jede Woche bekomme ich viele Hausaufgaben. — *I get no homework every month.*

....

4 Ich finde Chemie leicht, weil es interessant ist. — *I find chemistry hard because it's interesting.*

....

5 Zur Schule habe ich einen weißen Rock und ein schwarzes T-Shirt getragen. — *I wore a blue skirt and a grey T-shirt to school.*

....

3 Translate these sentences into English.

1 Ich mag Rock.

....

2 Dieses Lied ist lustig, denn es ist sehr schnell.

....

3 Jedes Jahr bekommen wir von der Schule die Noten.

....

4 Ich finde Mathe schwierig, weil es kompliziert ist.

....

5 Zur Schule habe ich eine blaue Hose und ein grünes Hemd getragen.

....

English to German

1 Draw lines to match up the English sentences with their German translations.

1 At school I like the canteen.

2 At home I love literature because it's complicated.

3 My favourite technology is my mobile phone because I listen to music.

4 I would like to buy a new laptop because my laptop is old.

5 At the weekend I wore a green dress and white shoes.

a *Zu Hause liebe ich Literatur, weil sie kompliziert ist.*

b *Ich möchte ein neues Laptop kaufen, weil mein Laptop alt ist.*

c *In der Schule mag ich die Kantine.*

d *Am Wochenende habe ich ein grünes Kleid und weiße Schuhe getragen.*

e *Meine Lieblingstechnologie ist mein Handy, denn ich höre Musik.*

2 Rewrite each German translation, putting the words into the correct order.

Remember to:
- put a capital letter on the first word of the German sentence
- add commas where needed
- add a full stop at the end.

1 I like streaming music. — *Musik streame gern ich*

....

2 I love social media because it's fast. — *schnell sind denn liebe ich sozialen die sie Medien*

....

3 My favourite technology is my laptop because it's really great. — *meine weil toll ist es mein Lieblingstechnologie Laptop ist wirklich*

....

4 I would like to buy a new novel at the weekend. — *Wochenende am ich möchte neuen kaufen einen Roman*

....

5 I wore a blue dress and black shoes to school. — *habe getragen ich blaues Kleid ein schwarze Schuhe und Schule zur*

....

3 Translate these sentences into German.

1 I like cooking.

....

2 I love pop music because it's loud.

....

3 My favourite technology is my smartphone because it's necessary and important.

....

4 I would like to buy a new phone because my phone is old.

....

5 At the weekend I wore a red skirt and a yellow T-shirt.

....

Higher translation revision

German to English

1 Complete the English translations.

1 Ich laufe jeden Tag, weil ich das mag.	*I .... every day because I .... it.*
2 Ich finde diese Musik sehr entspannend, denn sie ist leise.	*I find this music very .... because it's ....*
3 Dieser Star ist auf der Welt bekannt und er spielt in guten Filmen.	*This star is .... in the world and .... in good films.*
4 Ich habe das schwierig gefunden.	*I .... that ....*
5 In der Schule mag ich die Schulregeln nicht, weil sie zu nutzlos sind.	*At school I don't like the .... because they are .... useless.*

2 Translate the words in brackets into English to complete these sentences.

1 I paint every day, ... (*weil das leicht ist*)

2 I find sport very boring, ... (*denn das ist schwierig*)

3 This star is great, ... (*weil sie super ist*)

4 .... watched a new series. (*Ich habe*)

5 At school I don't like the school rules, ... (*denn sie sind verrückt*)

3 Translate these sentences into English.

1 Ich zeichne jede Woche, weil das entspannend ist.

....

2 Ich finde Musik sehr nützlich, denn man kann seine Probleme vergessen.

....

3 Dieser Sänger ist auf der Welt ziemlich unbekannt, aber er singt schöne Lieder.

....

4 Ich habe gute Noten bekommen. ....

5 In der Schule mag ich die Schuluniform überhaupt nicht, weil sie unbequem und nicht praktisch ist. ....

....

English to German

1 Colour one box from each column to translate each sentence into German. Use a different colour for each sentence. Then write out your translations.

Man	darf man	sehr	bekommen.
Es	singe	mit meiner Schwester	ein Konzert.
Ich	gehen wir	Computerprobleme	benutzen.
Heute Abend	klingt	in	kompliziert.
In der Schule	kann	das Handy	in einer Band.

1 I sing in a band with my sister. ....

2 You can get computer problems. ....

3 At school we are allowed to use mobile phones. ....

4 It sounds very complicated. ....

5 This evening we're going to a concert. ....

2 Translate the sentences into German, using the first letter of each word to help you.

1 I am actually a fan of this singer.

I | b | e | e | F | v | d | S.

2 One advantage is the contact with family.

E | V | i | d | K | m | d | F.

3 We aren't allowed to eat in the classroom.

M | d | i | K | n | e.

4 It sounds very slow.

D | k | s | l.

5 This evening the concert begins at eight o'clock.

H | A | b | d | K | u | a | U.

3 Translate these sentences into German.

1 I actually perform in a group with my friends.

....

2 One important disadvantage of technology is bullying.

....

3 At school we aren't allowed to speak in class.

....

4 It sounds very strange, but it's quite an important rule.

....

5 This evening the film starts at seven o'clock, so do you want to come?

....

Kulturzone Feste in der deutschsprachigen Welt

Giving opinions and justifications

1 Draw lines to match up the German words with their English translations.

1 das Ausland	**a** market
2 das Fest	**b** festival, celebration
3 das Geschenk	**c** event
4 der Markt	**d** drink
5 der Künstler	**e** present
H 6 das Getränk	**f** artist
H 7 das Ereignis	**g** foreign countries, abroad

2 Fill in the missing words in German.

1 Die Kleidung ist .... (*colourful*).

2 In Österreich gibt es ein Sportfest in der .... (*nature*).

3 Am sechsten Dezember .... (*find*) die Kinder Geschenke zu Hause.

H 4 Der Karneval hat in den deutschen Ländern eine lange .... (*tradition*).

H 5 Das Oktoberfest ist ein ganz .... (*special*) Fest.

Use a range of structures to give your opinion and justify it:
***Ich finde** Wandern toll, **weil** ich die Natur mag.*
I find hiking great **because** I like nature.
***Meiner Meinung nach** ist das Lauffest schön, **weil** ich Sport mag.*
In my opinion, the running festival is great **because** I like sports.
*Der Markt **interessiert mich (nicht), weil** es (zu) viele Leute gibt.*
I'm **(not) interested in** the market **because** there are (too) many people.

3 Draw lines to match up the sentence halves.

1 Ich finde das Fest toll, weil die	**a** ich Fahrradfahren mag.
2 Meiner Meinung nach ist der Markt teuer, weil	**b** das Essen zu viel kostet.
3 Das Straßenkunstfest interessiert mich, weil es	**c** Kleidung so schön und bunt ist.
4 Ich finde klassische Konzerte langweilig, weil ich	**d** Musik nicht mag.
5 Meiner Meinung nach ist das Fahrradsportfest wunderbar, weil	**e** viele Künstler dort gibt.

4 Rewrite each sentence, putting the word groups into the correct order.

1 den Markt schlecht, / es zu viele Leute gibt. / Ich finde / weil

....

2 wunderbar, / Ich finde / weil ich Geschenke / mag. / den sechsten Dezember

....

3 ist das Oktoberfest / Meiner Meinung / ich gern tanze. / nach / schön, weil

....

4 in der Natur ist. / man hier / weil / das Fest / Ich finde / interessant,

....

5 weil mir Schwimmen / Winterschwimmen interessiert / keinen Spaß macht. / mich nicht,

....

H 6 weil / ist Karneval toll, / Meiner Meinung nach / die Leute viel lachen.

....

H 5 Separate out the words and write out the German sentences. Remember to add capital letters to the nouns and a comma before *weil*.

1 Ichfindedenkarnevalschlechtweileseinemengeleutegibt.

....

2 Dasstraßenkunstfestinteressiertmichweilmankünstlerausallerweltsehenkann.

....

3 Meinermeinungnachistdieveranstaltunginteressantweilmirkunstgutgefällt.

....

4 Dasoktoberfestinteressiertmichnichtweildiegetränkezuteuersind.

....

5 Dugefällstmirintraditionellerkleidungweilichbuntekleidungmag.

....

F 6 Translate these sentences into English on a separate sheet.

1 Im Winter schwimmen hier viele Leute im kalten Wasser.

2 Am 6. Dezember bekommen die Kinder viele kleine Geschenke.

3 Ich finde das Fest wunderbar, weil ich Sport mag.

4 Der Markt ist toll, weil das Essen hier lecker ist.

5 Meiner Meinung nach ist das Oktoberfest interessant, weil man traditionelle Kleidung sieht.

H 7 Translate these sentences into German on a separate sheet.

1 In summer the street art festival takes place here.

2 The event lasts two days.

3 In my opinion the festival is great, because there are delicious food and great drinks.

4 I find Carnival fantastic because you can laugh and dance a lot.

5 The market does not interest me because it is expensive and noisy.

1 Wie ist deine Familie?

Using possessive adjectives • Using relative pronouns

1 Match up the German words with their English translations. Write the correct letter.

1 das Pferd ....
2 der Bruder ....
3 die Eltern ....
4 die Großeltern ....
5 die Tante ....
6 die Geschwister ....
H 7 die Brille ....

a siblings
b parents
c aunt
d grandparents
e horse
f glasses
g brother

2 Complete each sentence using a word from the box.

lächelt Brille Einzelkind Eigenschaften heißt kennst anders Haare

1 Mein Bruder ist mir nicht ähnlich, er ist ganz ....
2 Meine Mutter hat kurze weiße .... und ist ziemlich klein.
3 Ich habe keine Geschwister, ich bin ....
4 Mein Fisch .... Steven und ist total sportlich.
5 Unsere Katze ist immer freundlich und .... oft.
6 Meine Schwester, die du gut ...., ist nie böse.
H 7 Meine Oma ist nicht groß und trägt eine ....
H 8 Mein Opa ist 85 Jahre alt und hat viele gute ....

Look up unfamiliar words in the glossary at the end of the module and try to learn them.

3 Complete this text with the correct form of the possessive adjective (*mein*, *meine* or *meinen*).

1 .... Name ist Erik und ich wohne jetzt mit meiner Cousine zusammen in Wien.
2 .... Cousine heißt Susanne und ist total freundlich.
3 .... Brüder Tim und Anton sind noch klein und wohnen bei unseren Eltern in Köln.
4 .... Vater heißt Martin und er ist sehr freundlich.
5 .... Mutter heißt Luise und sie ist immer total lieb!
6 Ich liebe .... Eltern sehr! Sie haben eine gute Ehe und streiten nie. Wir haben auch Tiere.
7 Ich mag .... Katze sehr! Sie heißt Minka und schläft viel.
8 Ich liebe auch .... Fisch, aber er ist ab und zu traurig.
9 Aber .... Hund mag ich nicht. Er ist oft böse!

G

Possessive adjectives follow the same pattern as the indefinite article *ein*. Only the masculine form changes in the accusative. Remember that adjective endings need to agree with the noun they are describing.

	nominative (subject)	**accusative (object)**
masculine	mein (groß**er**) Bruder	mein**en** (groß**en**) Bruder
feminine	mein**e** (traurig**e**) Tante	mein**e** (traurig**e**) Tante
neuter	mein (grau**es**) Pferd	mein (grau**es**) Pferd
plural	mein**e** (lieb**en**) Eltern	mein**e** (lieb**en**) Eltern

These possessive adjectives also follow the same pattern:
dein (your – familiar, sg), ***sein*** (his), ***ihr*** (her), ***unser*** (our), ***eu(e)r*** (your – familiar, pl), ***Ihr*** (your – formal), ***ihr*** (their)

4 Complete these sentences with the correct possessive adjective.

1 .... (*her*) Onkel Hans ist geschieden.
2 .... (*his*) Tante Lisa ist sehr nett.
3 Frau Müller, wo leben .... (*your, formal*) Eltern?
4 Lena und Tim, ... (*your, informal pl*) Kinder sind sehr süß.
5 Tom besucht .... (*his*) Opa wenigstens zweimal im Jahr.
H 6 Karli, ... (*your*) Katze hat einen schlechten Charakter!

G

Relative pronouns (who, which) refer back to someone or something. They send the verb to the end of the clause.
Relative pronouns must be used in the same case as the noun to which they refer.
Subject (nom): ***Dein großer Bruder*, *der*** *Theo heißt, ist sehr lustig.* (Here, ***der*** (referring back to ***dein großer Bruder***) is the subject of the relative clause.)
H **Object (acc): Dein großer Bruder, den** ich sehr mag, ist lustig. (Here, *ich* is the subject and ***den*** is the object of the relative clause.)

	German	English
masc.	Mein (großer) Bruder, ***der*** ...	My (big) brother, **who** ...
fem.	Meine (traurige) Tante, ***die*** ...	My (sad) aunt, **who** ...
neuter	Mein (graues) Pferd, ***das*** ...	My (grey) horse, **which** ...
plural	Meine (lieben) Eltern, ***die*** ...	My (dear) parents, **who** ...

H **5 Circle the correct relative pronoun to complete each sentence.**

1 Unsere Geschwister, **der / die / das** immer gute Laune haben, wohnen in Berlin.
2 Dein Bruder, **der / das / den** eine Tätowierung hat, ist ledig.
3 Sein Onkel, **der / das / den** ich nicht kenne, ist sehr eifersüchtig.
4 Ihre Tante, **die / das / den** nicht verheiratet ist, lebt in einer zivilen Partnerschaft.
5 Eure Oma, **der / die / das** keine Brille trägt, hat blaue Augen.
6 Euer Vogel, **der / die / das** ziemlich hübsch ist, ist manchmal traurig.

F **6 Translate these sentences into German on a separate sheet.**

1 My cousin Jens is quite small.
2 I find my dog, who is called Adam, totally sweet!
3 Do you know my stepbrother who lives in London?
4 Her horse, which is black and white, is nine years old.
5 His girlfriend, who is totally friendly, is divorced.

This word may be unfamiliar but it has appeared in German in a previous exercise in this unit. Did you look it up when you came across it?

H **7 Translate these sentences into English on a separate sheet.**

1 Mein Name ist Henry und auf dem Foto sieht man meine Familie.
2 Mein Onkel, der in Wien wohnt, trägt eine Brille.
3 Meine Stiefmutter, die schwarze Haare hat, ist sehr großzügig.
4 Mein Vater, der nie böse ist, hat kurze rote Haare.
5 Unser Pferd, das Pedro heißt, ist sehr hübsch.

Using pronouns and possessive adjectives in the dative

1 Fill in the missing letters.

1 Fre_n_in

2 H_l_br_der

3 To_ht_r

4 On_el

5 T_n_e

6 B_zie_ung

2 Underline the adjective(s) in each sentence and translate it/them into English.

1 Wer ist ganz sportlich? ....

2 Mein Sohn ist oft faul und das ist ärgerlich. ....

3 Unser Opa ist wirklich streng. ....

H 4 Unsere Tochter und unser Sohn sind sehr unterschiedlich. ....

H 5 Unsere Oma ist total nett und großzügig. ....

H 6 Meine Stiefschwester ist absolut unabhängig. ....

G

Some prepositions, like *mit* (with), are always followed by **dative** pronouns or possessive adjectives.
Ich verstehe mich (nicht) gut ***mit*** ... I (don't) get on well **with**...

masculine	mein**em** Bruder	**ihm**
feminine	mein**er** Tante	**ihr**
neuter	mein**em** Kind	**ihm**
plural	mein**en** Eltern	**H ihnen**

3 Circle the correct dative possessive adjectives to complete each sentence.

1 Ich verstehe mich gut mit **meiner** / **meinem** / **meinen** Sohn.

2 Verstehst du dich gut mit **deiner** / **deinem** / **deinen** Eltern?

3 Ich verstehe mich gut mit **meiner** / **meinem** / **meinen** Kind.

4 Ich verstehe mich nicht gut mit **meiner** / **meinem** / **meinen** Stiefmutter.

5 Aber ich verstehe mich sehr gut mit **meiner** / **meinem** / **meinen** Tante.

4 Complete these sentences with the correct dative pronoun.

1 Meine Mutter ist freundlich und geduldig und ich verstehe mich mit gut mit ....

2 Dein Bruder ist sehr hilfsbereit und höflich. Verstehst du dich gut mit ....?

3 Ich glaube fest an ihn, denn ich verstehe mich gut mit ....

H 4 Meine Großeltern sind zu ernst und ich komme nicht so gut mit .... aus.

H 5 Meine Schwester ist oft frech und gemein und ich komme nicht gut mit .... aus.

5 Complete these sentences with the correct pronoun from the box to replace the underlined words.

ihm ihr ihm
H uns H ihnen H euch

1 Ich spiele mit <u>meinem Pferd</u>.

Ich spiele mit ....

2 Ich verstehe mich gut mit <u>meinem Opa</u>.

Ich verstehe mich gut mit ....

3 Ich gehe mit <u>meiner Freundin</u> spazieren.

Ich gehe mit .... spazieren.

H 4 Kommst du <u>mit Daniel und mir</u> ins Kino?

Kommst du mit .... ins Kino?

H 5 Ich war zusammen mit <u>meinen Freundinnen</u> auf dem Fest.

Ich war zusammen mit .... auf dem Fest.

H 6 Ich fahre mit <u>dir und deiner Tante</u> nach Berlin.

Ich fahre mit .... nach Berlin.

G

nominative	dative
ich	mir
du	dir
er	ihm
sie	ihr
es	ihm
wir	H uns
ihr	H euch
Sie	Ihnen
sie	H ihnen

F **6 Translate these sentences into English.**

1 Wir haben dieselben Interessen.

....

2 Mein Bruder geht mir oft auf die Nerven.

....

3 Du bist sehr aktiv und ich spiele oft Fußball mit dir.

....

4 Ich verstehe mich nicht so gut mit deinem Freund, denn er ist immer so blöd.

....

5 Frau Müller, Sie sind so ehrlich und ich verstehe mich wirklich gut mit Ihnen!

....

H **7 Translate these sentences into German.**

1 Do you get on well with your family?

....

2 My father is always totally strict.

....

3 My sister and I have different interests.

....

4 I have a very good relationship with my stepmother because she is very generous.

....

5 My brother often gets on my nerves, but that's normal!

....

3 Wer ist dir wichtig?

- Using two time frames together: past and present
- Word order with *da* and *weil*

1 Unjumble the letters to rewrite the words correctly.

1 ertiewlvn ....

2 nersöchPlikeit ....

3 mDea ....

H 4 feEktf ....

H 5 nscEehaigft ....

2 Underline the noun(s) in each sentence and translate them into English on a separate sheet.

1 Die Situation ist mir nicht egal.

2 Sie hat viel für die Rechte von Menschen gemacht, zum Beispiel für die, die bisexuell sind.

H 3 Oft sind solche Probleme immer noch ein Teil von ihrem Leben.

H 4 Sie bringt große Opfer und der Kampf für Kinder ist total wichtig für sie.

H 5 Er ist ein ungewöhnlicher Typ und ein Vorbild für die Jugend, denn er kämpft für eine bessere Welt.

G

Use the present and past tenses alongside each other to add interest and complexity to your German.

*Sie **ist** eine tolle Persönlichkeit und **hat** immer viel für Kinder **gemacht**.*

She **is** a great celebrity and **has** always **done** a lot for children.

Remember:

- In the **perfect tense**, verbs involving **movement** or a **change of state** take ***sein***.
- The **past participle for regular verbs** is formed by adding ***ge-*** and ***-t*** to the verb stem.
- Some irregular verbs add -***en*** instead of ***-t*** and others have a vowel change or are completely irregular:

gesehen → *Du hast den Film geseh**en**.* You saw the film.

gewinnen → *Er hat den Song Contest gew**o**nnen.* He won the Song Contest.

H *kennen* → *Ich habe das Lied vorher nicht gek**a**nn**t**.* I did not know the song before.

3 Write the correct tense (past (P) or present (Pr)) for each sentence. Then translate the sentences into English.

1 Er hat viel im Leben erfahren. ☐

....

2 Stars sind für mich nie wichtig gewesen. ☐

....

3 Meine Tante ist eine tolle Dame, weil sie sehr kreativ ist. ☐

....

H 4 Er hat einen sehr positiven Einfluss und viele Menschen vertrauen ihm. ☐

....

H 5 Deshalb müssen wir uns gegenseitig akzeptieren. ☐

....

H 6 Ihre ständige Arbeit in der Organisation ist hilfreich und hat einen positiven Effekt auf die Welt. ☐

....

4 Complete these sentences with the correct tense of the verb in brackets.

1 Er .... alle Leute und .... vielen Menschen. (*akzeptieren* – present, *helfen* – present)

2 Stars .... mir egal und für mich .... Persönlichkeiten noch nie wichtig .... (*sein* – present, *sein* – perfect)

3 Paula .... bei einer Zeitung und .... ein Interview mit einem bisexuellen Paar .... (*arbeiten* – present, *machen* – perfect)

4 Damals .... mein Bruder heterosexuell ...., aber heute .... er bisexuell. (*sein* – perfect, *sein* – present)

H 5 Einige Leute .... sich nun in Deutschland nicht .... (*wohlfühlen* (separable verb) – present)

H 5 Rewrite each sentence on a separate sheet, putting the word groups into the correct order.

1 Ich habe sie immer toll gefunden, / zwischen arm und reich macht. / weil sie keinen Unterschied

2 immer unterstützt hat. / Meine Halbschwester / da sie mich / ist mir wichtig,

3 weil er viel erlebt hat. / Ich habe meinen Opa / immer interessant gefunden,

4 meine Oma wunderbar, / Ich finde / weil sie ein hohes Alter hat.

5 da sie in einer anderen Wirklichkeit leben. / immer langweilig gefunden, / Ich habe Stars

> **G**
> Remember that ***da*** and ***weil*** send the verb to the end of the sentence or clause.
> *Mein Opa ist mir immer wichtig,* ***weil*** *er mich immer unterstützt* ***hat****.*
> *Stars sind mir noch nie wichtig gewesen,* ***da*** *sie nicht in einer echten Welt* ***leben****.*

F 6 Translate these sentences into German on a separate sheet.

1 I find stars boring.

2 My aunt is very important to me.

3 She is successful because she works hard.

4 My uncle is great because he helps a lot of people.

5 I think my mother is patient and she has always understood me.

H 7 Translate these sentences into English on a separate sheet.

1 Mein Vater hat immer für das Volk gekämpft.

2 Er hat auf die Probleme der Kinder reagiert.

3 So ist eine Organisation entstanden, die Kindern hilft.

> This is the past participle of *entstehen*.

4 Ich finde auch, dass jede Person einzeln und individuell helfen kann.

5 Meiner Meinung nach sind Vorbilder wichtig, weil sie vielen Menschen helfen.

4 Wir haben gefeiert!
Practising word order

1 Translate these words into English.

1 der Geburtstag ....
2 die Ferien ....
3 der Anfang ....
4 die Hochzeit ....
5 der Strand ....
H 6 das Feuerwerk ....

2 Complete these sentences by translating the verbs in brackets into German.

1 Am Wochenende bin ich mit meiner Freundin ins Kino
.... (*gone*)

2 Letzte Woche habe ich mit meiner Freundin, die Jüdin ist, das neue Jahr
.... (*celebrated*)

3 Am Wochenende hat Murat nochmal etwas über Eid
.... (*told*)

H 4 Am Anfang .... ein großes Feuer auf dem Berg. (*there was*)

3 Rewrite these sentences, adding the adverbial phrase in brackets in the correct position.

1 Wir waren auf dem Fest. (*am Wochenende*)

....

2 Ich bin am Nachmittag auf den Markt gegangen. (*mit meinem Bruder*)

....

....

3 Ich habe mit meiner Familie gefeiert. (*bei meinen Großeltern*)

....

....

G
Remember the word order rule: **time** (when) – ***manner*** (how) – **place** (where):
Ich habe **letztes Jahr** *Karneval* ***mit meinen Freunden*** **in Köln** *gefeiert.*
Remember that the verb always stays in second position:
Im Dezember habe ich Silvester mit meiner Familie zu Hause gefeiert.

H 4 Ich habe am Samstag den Ausdruck „Herzlichen Glückwunsch" gesagt. (*im Restaurant*)

....

....

4 Rewrite these sentences using the correct word order. Keep the underlined word group first.

1 Wir haben / meinen Geburtstag / gefeiert / im Park / letzten Freitag

....

2 Nach den Prüfungen / mit meiner Freundin / habe ich / gegessen / am Strand

....

3 Anja und Peter / gefahren / mit dem Zug / zum Oktoberfest / sind letzte Woche

....

Remember that the place comes last, just before the past participle.

H **4** <u>Lise ist</u> / mit ihrem Freund / auf den Karneval / gegangen / neulich

....

H **5** <u>Ich habe</u> / meine Prüfung bestanden und habe deshalb / im Stadtzentrum / gefeiert / am Freitag / mit meinen Großeltern

....

H **5 Write full sentences to answer these questions, using the correct word order and the phrases in brackets.**

Wann, mit wem und wo hast du ...

1 ... ein Musikfest besucht? (*im Dorf, am Samstag, mit meinen Geschwistern*)

....

2 ... Geburtstag gefeiert? (*mit meinem Bruder, am Strand, im August*)

....

3 ... eine Party organisiert? (*im Restaurant, mit meinem Onkel, am Samstag*)

....

4 ... ein großes Feuerwerk gesehen? (*im Stadtzentrum, am Wochenende, mit meiner Freundin*)

....

F **6 Translate these sentences into English.**

1 Auf dem Fest feiern Christen, Hindus, Muslime und Juden zusammen.

....

2 Auf der Hochzeit haben wir viel Spaß gehabt.

....

3 An Eid habe ich mit meiner Familie zu Hause viel gegessen und getrunken.

....

4 Ich habe in den Ferien mit meinen Eltern einen tollen Film im Kino gesehen.

....

5 Ich habe an Silvester in Köln getanzt, gelacht und viele nette Leute kennengelernt.

....

H **7 Translate these sentences into German.**

1 Last month, I went to the famous Oktoberfest.

....

2 The festival takes place annually in Munich.

....

3 I really enjoyed the festival and the atmosphere was fantastic!

....

4 We had a lot of fun and laughed, danced and sang the whole day.

....

5 We also ate too much and met nice people.

....

5 Partyzeit!

- Using two time frames together: past and future
- Using *in* + accusative or dative

1 Translate these words into German. Include the definite article (*der*, *die* or *das*).

1 cake ....

2 cinema ....

3 classroom ....

4 sports centre ....

5 city centre ....

2 Complete each sentence using a verb from the box.

hören	lesen
gefeiert	gelacht
sehen	gemacht

1 Am Mittwoch habe ich mit meinen Freunden im Garten eine Party

....

2 Wir haben den Anfang der Ferien ....

3 Wir haben viel gegessen, getanzt und ....

4 In den Ferien werde ich viel schlafen und Musik ....

5 Ich werde auch ins Kino gehen und Filme ....

6 Natürlich werde ich in den Ferien auch Bücher ....

G

To add interest and complexity to your German, use the **past** and **future** tenses in your work.

Past	Future
Ich ***habe*** *eine Geburtstagsparty* ***geplant****.*	*Ich* ***werde*** *eine Geburtstagsparty* ***planen****.*
Das ***hat*** *viel Spaß* ***gemacht****.*	*Das* ***wird*** *viel Spaß* ***machen****.*
Auf der Party ***haben*** *wir viel Kuchen* ***gegessen****.*	*Auf der Party* ***werden*** *wir viel Kuchen* ***essen****.*
Die Party ***hat*** *im Sportzentrum* ***stattgefunden****.*	*Die Party* ***wird*** *im Sportzentrum* ***stattfinden****.*

3 Circle the correct form of the verb to complete each sentence.

To help you decide which tense is needed, look at the time expressions, and whether a past participle or infinitive is used at the end of the sentence.

1 Letztes Wochenende **hat** / **wird** meine Tante geheiratet.

2 Am Montag **haben** / **werden** wir den Anfang der Ferien feiern.

3 Am Sonntag **habe** / **werde** ich mit meinen Eltern zu Hause essen.

4 Wir **haben** / **werden** ein Spiel gespielt, viel gelacht und Cola getrunken.

5 Nächsten Monat **habe** / **werde** ich mit meiner Familie nach Berlin fahren.

4 Rewrite these perfect tense sentences in the future tense.

1 Ich habe am Wochenende eine Geburtstagsparty gemacht. ....

....

2 Ich habe viele schöne Geschenke bekommen. ....

....

3 Ich habe dich eingeladen und meinen Kuchen mit dir geteilt. ....

....

4 Meine Oma hat mich mit einem leckeren Kuchen überrascht. ....

....

5 Aber mein Bruder hat sich nicht an meinen Geburtstag erinnert. ....

....

Some prepositions such as ***in*** can be followed by either the **accusative** case (indicating **movement**) or the **dative** case (indicating **position**). **G**

		masculine	feminine	neuter	plural
accusative (movement)	ich gehe **in**	**den** Garten	**die** Schule	**das** Restaurant	**die** Geschäfte
dative (position)	ich bin **in**	**dem** Garten	**der** Schule	**dem** Restaurant	**den** Geschäften

in dem is often abbreviated to ***im***. ***in das*** is often abbreviated to ***ins***.

5 Complete these sentences with the correct form of the definite article.

1 Am Wochenende werde ich mit Freunden in .... Park (*m*) gehen.

2 Im Sommer sind wir oft in .... Sportzentrum (*nt*) gegangen.

3 Am Samstag werde ich in .... Stadtmitte (*f*) gehen und einen Kuchen kaufen.

4 In .... Restaurants (*pl*) haben viele Leute ihren Geburtstag gefeiert.

5 Wir waren in .... Schule (*f*) und haben den Anfang der Ferien gefeiert.

6 In .... Klassenzimmer (*nt*) gab es viele Geschenke.

F 6 Translate these sentences into German.

1 My parents celebrate their wedding at the restaurant.

....

2 Last week I celebrated my birthday in the garden.

....

3 On Saturday we will go into town.

....

4 Yesterday I studied a lot but in the holidays I will be in the park.

....

5 On Monday I was in the cinema but on Wednesday I will go to the restaurant.

....

H 7 Translate these sentences into English on a separate sheet.

1 Ich habe eine Geburtstagsparty für meinen Cousin organisiert.

2 Er war total überrascht, weil ich ihm vorher nichts gesagt habe.

3 Die Feier hat im Haus stattgefunden und das war wunderbar.

4 Im Juli werde ich eine Party für meinen Onkel machen.

5 Wo die Feier stattfinden wird, wird vom Wetter abhängen.

Glossary

bold = this word will appear in Higher exams only

abhängen	(to) depend / depending
absolut	absolute, complete, absolutely, completely
ähnlich	similar, similarly
aktiv	active, energetic
akzeptieren	(to) accept / accepting
alt	old
Alter (nt)	age
andere (r, s)	other, different
anders	different, differently
Anfang (m)	beginning, start
ärgerlich	annoying, irritating
Ausdruck (m)	term, expression
auskommen (mit)	(to) get on with / getting on with
Ausland (nt)	foreign countries, abroad
Beispiel (nt)	example, instance
besondere (r, s)	special
Beziehung (f)	relation, relationship
bi(sexuell)	bi, bisexual
bist	(you (sing informal)) are / are being
blöd	stupid, dumb
böse	bad, mad, naughty, angry
Brille (f)	glasses, pair of glasses
Bruder (m)	brother
Brüder (pl)	brothers
bunt	colourful, colourfully
Charakter (m)	character
Christ (m)	Christian
Cousin (m)	cousin (male)
Cousine (f)	cousin (female)
damals	then, at that time, in those days
Dame (f)	lady
das	the; which (nt), that
dein	your (m, nt)
deine	your (f, pl)
der	the; which (m)
deshalb	therefore
dich	you (obj) / yourself (reflex)
die	the; which (f, pl)
dir	(to) you (indirect obj)
Effekt (m)	effect
egal	(it's all) the same, indifferent, doesn't matter
Ehe (f)	marriage
ehrlich	honest
eifersüchtig	jealous
Eigenschaft (f)	quality, characteristic, trait
Einfluss (m)	influence
einladen	(to) invite / inviting
Einzelkind (nt)	only child
einzeln	individual, single, separately
Eltern (pl)	(pl) parents
entstehen	(to) originate, develop / originating, developing
Ereignis (nt)	event, occurrence, incident
erfahren	(to) experience, find out / experiencing, finding out

erinnern (an acc. + noun); sich erinnern (an acc. + noun)	*(to) remind (about + noun) | reminding (about + noun); (to) remember (+ noun) | remembering (+ noun)*
erleben	*(to) experience | experiencing*
ernst	*serious*
erzählen (von + noun)	*(to) tell (about + noun) | telling (about + noun)*
es (…) gab	*there was / there were / there used to be*
es ist mir egal	*I don't care*
euch	***(to) you (pl informal) (obj)** | yourselves (informal) (reflex) / each other (informal) (reciprocal)*
euer	*your (informal, pl) (m, nt)*
eure	*your (informal, pl) (f, pl)*
Familie (f)	*family*
faul	*lazy, idle*
Feier (f)	*celebration, party, ceremony*
feiern	*(to) celebrate, party | celebrating, partying*
Ferien (pl)	*holidays, school break (pl)*
fest	*firm, solid, steady*
Fest (nt)	*festival, celebration*
Feuer (nt)	*fire, bonfire*
Feuerwerk (nt)	*fireworks*
Fisch (m)	*fish*
frech	*cheeky, naughty*
Freund (m)	*friend*
freundlich	*kind, nice, friendly*
Geburtstag (m)	*birthday*
geduldig	*patient*
gefallen	*(to) please | pleasing*
(aux)…gegangen	*went / (have, has) gone (pp)*
gegenseitig	*mutual, each other*
(aux)…gegessen	*ate / (have, has) eaten (pp)*
(aux)…gekannt	*knew / (have, has) known (pp)*
gemein	*mean, cruel, nasty*
Geschenk (nt)	*gift, present*
geschieden	*divorced*
Geschwister (pl)	*(pl) siblings*
Getränk (nt)	*drink*
(aux)…gewesen	*was | (have, has) been (pp)*
(aux)…gewonnen	*won | (have, has) won (pp)*
groß	*big, tall, great*
Großeltern (pl)	*grandparents*
großzügig	*generous*
gute / schlechte Laune haben	*(to) be in a good/ bad mood | being in a good/ bad mood*
Haar (nt)	*hair*
heißen	*(to) be called*
Herzlichen Glückwunsch (zum Geburtstag)	*congratulations (Happy Birthday)*
hetero(sexuell)	*straight, heterosexual*
hier	*here*
hilfreich	*helpful*
hilfsbereit	*helpful, co-operative*
Hindu (m) (f)	*Hindu*
Hochzeit (f)	*wedding, marriage*
höflich	*polite*
hübsch	*pretty, cute, lovely*
Hund (m)	*dog*

ihm	*(to) him / it (m, nt) (indirect obj)*
ihn	*him / it (m) (obj)*
Ihnen	*(to) you (formal, indirect obj)*
Ihnen	*(to) them*
ihr	*her, its, their (m, nt)*
ihr	*you (pl informal) (subj) | (to) her, to it (f) (indirect obj)*
ihre	*her, its, their (f, pl)*
individuell	*individual, individually*
Interesse (nt)	*interest*
Interview (nt)	*interview*
jährlich	*annually*
jdm auf die Nerven gehen	*(to) get on someone's nerves | getting on someone's nerves*
Jude (m)	*Jewish person (m)*
Jüdin (f)	*Jewish person (f)*
Jugend (f)	*youth*
Kampf (m)	*fight, struggle, battle*
kämpfen	*(to) fight, struggle, battle | fighting, struggling, battling*
Katze (f)	*cat*
kennen	*(to) know | knowing*
klein	*small, little, short (of a person)*
Kuchen (m)	*cake*
Künstler (m)	*artist, performer*
kurz	*short, brief*
lächeln	*(to) smile | smiling*
lachen	*(to) laugh | laughing*
ledig	*single, unmarried*
Leute (pl)	*(pl) people*
lieb	*dear, kind*
meiner Meinung nach	*in my opinion*
Meinung (f)	*opinion, view*
Menge (f)	*quantity, amount, a lot of, crowd (people)*
Mensch (m)	*human being, person*
mich	*me (obj) / myself (reflex)*
mir	*(to) me (indirect obj)*
Muslim(e) (m) (f)	*Muslim*
Mutter (f)	*mother*
Name (m)	*name*
Natur (f)	*nature*
nett	*nice*
neulich	*recently, the other day, lately*
nochmal	*again*
normal	*normal*
nun	*now, well*
Oma (f)	*grandma, grandmother*
Onkel (m)	*uncle*
Opa (m)	*grandpa, grandad, grandfather*
Opfer (nt)	*sacrifice, victim, casualty*
organisieren	*(to) organise | organising*
Paar (nt)	*pair, couple*
Persönlichkeit (f)	*personality, celebrity*
Problem (nt)	*problem*
reagieren (auf acc. + noun)	*(to) react (to + noun) | reacting (to + noun)*
Recht (nt)	*right, law*
schlecht	*bad, badly*
Schwester (f)	*sister*
sein	*his, its (m, nt)*

seine	*his, its (f, pl)*
Situation (f)	*situation*
Sohn (m)	*son*
solch	*such*
sportlich	*sporty, athletic*
ständig	*constant, permanent, constantly, permanently*
stattfinden	*(to) take place, occur / taking place, occurring*
Stief-	*step-*
streiten	*(to) quarrel, argue, dispute / quarrelling, arguing, disputing*
streng	*strict, severe*
süß	*sweet, sugary, cute*
Tante (f)	*aunt*
Tätowierung (f)	*tattoo, tattooing*
Teil (m) (nt)	*part, piece*
teilen	*(to) share, divide / sharing, dividing*
Tochter (f)	*daughter*
Tradition (f)	*tradition*
Typ (m)	*bloke, guy*
überraschen	*(to) surprise / surprising*
unabhängig	*independent*
ungewöhnlich	*unusual, unusually*
uns	***(to) us (obj)** / ourselves (reflex) / each other (recip)*
unser	*our (m, nt)*
unsere	*our (f, pl)*
Unterschied (m)	*difference*
unterschiedlich	*different, varied, variable, diverse*
unterstützen	*(to) support / supporting*
Vater (m)	*father*
Veranstaltung (f)	*event, performance*
verheiratet	*married*
vertrauen	*(to) trust / trusting*
Vogel (m)	*bird*
Volk (nt)	*people*
Vorbild (nt)	*role model, example*
vorher	*earlier, beforehand, previously*
wenigstens	*at least*
wer?	*who?*
Werk (nt)	*work, plant, factory*
Wirklichkeit (f)	*reality, truth*
wohl	*well, probably, arguably*
zivile Partnerschaft (f)	*civil partnership*
zusammen	*together, altogether*

Kulturzone Ich liebe Sport

- Using comparative adjectives and adverbs
- **H** Using superlative adjectives and adverbs

1 Translate these German adjectives into English.

1 gut ....
4 nah near............................
7 jung ....
2 hoch ....
5 oft ....
8 schwach ....
3 groß ....
6 alt ....
9 stark ....

2 Complete each sentence using a word from the box.

Sport Fahrrad Bergen Basketball Fitness-Studio

1 Ich laufe gern und fahre oft ....
2 Mia spielt gern Fußball, aber sie spielt auch ab und zu ....
3 Tom geht im Sommer schwimmen, aber im Winter geht er ins ....
4 Ich treibe regelmäßig .... und spiele im Sommer oft Tennis.
H **5** Aisha geht im Sommer manchmal in den .... wandern.

G

The **comparative** is used to **compare** two things: just add **-er** to the adjective/adverb and use ***als*** to mean 'than'.

klein – small *klein**er*** – small**er**

*Die Schweiz ist kleiner **als** Österreich.*

Switzerland is smaller **than** Austria.

Some adjectives are **irregular**:
gut – ***besser,*** *viel* – ***mehr***,
gern – ***lieber***, *hoch* – ***höher***.

One-syllable adjectives often add an umlaut: *groß* – ***größer***, *nah* – ***näher***, *oft* – ***öfter***.

Remember that adjectives need to agree with the noun they are describing:

*Skifahren ist ein gefährlich**erer** Sport als Tennis.*

G

H The **superlative** is used to say something is 'the most …': add ***-(e)st*** at the end of the adjective and make sure it agrees with the noun.

*Für die Schweizer ist Wandern der beliebte**ste** Sport.*

For the Swiss, hiking is the **most popular** sport.

Remember that some adjectives are **irregular** (*der/die/das beste …; der/die/das meiste …*) and one-syllable adjectives often add an umlaut (*der/die/das n**ä**chste*).

*Was ist die größ**te** Zahl?*
What is the biggest number?

For superlatives on their own, without a noun after them, use ***am*** before the adjective and add ***-(e)sten*** at the end.

*Dieser Berg ist **am** höch**sten**.*
This mountain is the highest.

*Dieses Hotel ist **am** näch**sten**.*
This hotel is the nearest.

3 Circle the correct adjective/adverb to complete each sentence.

1 Im Sommer ist es **warm** / **wärmer** als im Winter.
2 Ich finde Schwimmen **langweiliger** / **langweilig** als Fahrradfahren.
3 Im deutschen Raum ist Fahrradfahren **beliebt** / **beliebter** als Wandern.
4 Die Berge sind **näher** / **nah** an München als an Berlin.
5 Joggst du **lieber** / **gern** in der Natur oder im Fitness-Studio?

4 Complete these sentences with the correct German comparative form by translating the word(s) in brackets.

1 Ich möchte .... (*more often*) wandern gehen.

2 Die Berge in der Schweiz sind .... (*higher*) als in Deutschland.

3 Ich bin so schwach wie mein Bruder und unsere Schwester ist viel .... (*stronger*) als wir.

4 Ich spiele gut Tennis, aber ich spiele .... (*better*) Basketball.

5 Sie spielen viel Tennis, aber sie spielen .... (*more*) Fußball.

H 6 Ich fahre .... (*more frequently*) Fahrrad als meine Stiefschwester.

H 5 Complete each sentence using the correct comparative or superlative form of an adjective/adverb from the box.

hoch schnell gern lang jung

1 Mein .... Lauf war 20 Kilometer.

2 Mein Bruder Sven fährt mindestens dreimal in der Woche Fahrrad und fährt viel .... als ich.

3 Der .... Berg, der zu Deutschland gehört, heißt die *Zugspitze*.

4 Meine Schwester ist .... als ich und macht in meiner Familie am meisten Sport.

5 Ich gehe gern wandern, aber am .... gehe ich klettern.

F 6 Translate these sentences into German.

1 I find fitness training exciting. ....

2 In the winter it is colder than in the summer. ....

3 I find hiking more boring than cycling. ....

4 I play tennis well, but I play football better.

....

5 My brother is older than me and plays basketball often.

....

H 7 Translate these sentences into English.

1 Meine Familie ist sehr groß, denn wir sind fünf Kinder.

....

2 Meine jüngste Schwester findet Schwimmen spannender als Wandern.

....

3 Wir sind jeden Tag dreißig Kilometer Fahrrad gefahren!

....

4 Das war eine tolle Leistung, weil es auch der kälteste Sommer war!

....

5 Neulich bin ich mit meinem ältesten Bruder in den Schweizer Bergen klettern gegangen.

....

1 Willst du fit und gesund sein?

F Revising modal verbs

1 Underline the noun(s) in each sentence and translate them into English.

1 Ich habe immer großen Hunger und esse viel Käse.

....

2 Ich esse oft Brot mit Wurst und Ei. ....

3 Ich trinke nie Alkohol und rauche nie Zigaretten. ....

4 Ich trinke nie Bier oder Wein und ich nehme nie Drogen. ....

5 Ich esse nie Zucker, aber viel Obst und Gemüse. ....

To say 'I am hungry/thirsty' in German, you need to say 'I **have** hunger/thirst':
*Ich **habe** Hunger. Ich **habe** Durst.*

2 Circle the correct form of *mögen* to complete each sentence.

1 Ich habe Durst, aber ich **magst** / **mag** / **mögt** Wasser nicht.

2 Herr Zimmer **mögt** / **magst** / **mag** die Wurst auf dem Tisch nicht.

3 Einige Personen **mögt** / **mögen** / **mag** Eis nicht.

4 Frau Schneider, **mag** / **magst** / **mögen** Sie das Essen hier im Restaurant?

5 **Mögen** / **Mögt** / **Mag** ihr Hähnchen?

3 Complete these sentences with the correct form of the modal verb in brackets.

1 Sofia, ... du Kaffee? (*mögen*)

2 Ich .... gesund essen. (*wollen*)

3 Florian und Brigitte, ... ihr scharfes Essen? (*mögen*)

4 Du .... keine Drogen nehmen. (*sollen*)

5 Wie .... Sie zahlen? (*wollen*)

G

Remember that **modal verbs** are usually used with another verb in the infinitive form at the end of the sentence.
*Ich **will** keine Drogen nehmen.* I don't want to take drugs.
*Sie **sollen** gesund essen.* They **should** eat healthily.
mögen (to like) is a modal verb, but it is not always used with an infinitive. It is most commonly used with a noun.

mögen (*to like*)	
ich	mag
du	magst
er/sie/es/man	mag
wir	mögen
ihr	mögt
Sie	mögen
sie	mögen

*Ich **mag** Cola.* I like cola.
Remember, to say you like doing something, use ***gern*** after the verb.
*Ich trinke **gern** Cola.* I like drinking cola.

4 Translate these sentences into German.

Use the glossary at the end of the module to look up any words that are unfamiliar, and try to learn them.

1 I never want to smoke.

....

2 I don't like cigarettes because they are not healthy.

....

3 We should eat more vegetables.

....

4 I like cola, but I prefer to drink water.

....

5 The food in the restaurant was not good.

....

1 Willst du fit und gesund sein?

H Using *um ... zu*

H 1 Complete these German sentences by translating the words in brackets.

1 Er trinkt jetzt kaum Alkohol, zum Beispiel Bier, und ist nie .... (*drunk*)

2 Es ist nicht gesund, entweder zu dünn oder .... zu sein. (*overweight*)

3 Die Gerichte im Restaurant enthalten viel leckeres .... (*vegetables*)

4 .... hat viel Protein. (*milk*)

5 Drogen nehmen macht .... (*addicted*)

H 2 Separate out the words and write out the sentences on a separate sheet.

1 Ichmussnichtbetrunkenseinumspaßzuhaben.

2 Ichesserelativgesundumnichtübergewichtigzusein.

3 Manmussaufpassenumnichtsüchtigzusein.

4 Ichhabeeinentraineruminformzubleiben.

5 Stattfastfoodzuwählenesseichhähnchen.

Add a capital letter to each noun and a comma before *um*.

G

H Use the infinitive construction **um ... zu** to say '(in order) to'. The infinitive goes to the end of the clause and there is a comma before *um*:
Ich höre viel Musik, ***um*** *mich* ***zu entspannen****.* I listen to music a lot (**in order**) **to** relax.
ohne ... zu (without) and ***statt ... zu*** (instead of) are used in the same way:
Ich esse gesund, ***ohne*** *leckeres Essen auf****zu****geben.* I eat healthily without giving up tasty food.
Statt *Cola* ***zu*** *trinken, trinke ich Wasser.* Instead of drinking cola, I drink water.
With separable verbs, ***zu*** comes in the middle of the word, **after** the separable prefix.
*Ich plane, morgen früh auf****zu****stehen.* I plan to get up early tomorrow.

H 3 Write full sentences with the words in brackets, using *um ... zu, ohne ... zu* or *statt ... zu* + infinitive.

1 Ich telefoniere mit dem Restaurant, ... (*um gesundes Essen, bestellen*)

2 Ich mache viel Sport, ... (*um auf die Gesundheit, aufpassen*)

3 Ich esse gesund, ... (*ohne auf leckeres Essen, verzichten*)

4 Ich trinke Wein und so weiter nicht, ... (*um nicht betrunken, sein*)

5 Ich gehe jedes Wochenende schwimmen, ... (*statt auf Partys, gehen*)

H 4 Translate these sentences into German on a separate sheet.

1 I have some friends who smoke regularly.

2 I think that is extremely stupid because it's dangerous.

3 In order to live healthily, we do not take drugs.

4 Instead of partying with friends every weekend, we should relax more.

5 Next year I will jog three laps every day with a trainer!

eine Runde *a round, lap*

2 Es geht mir nicht gut

Using modal verbs in the imperfect tense

1 Match the English words with their German translations. Write the correct letter.

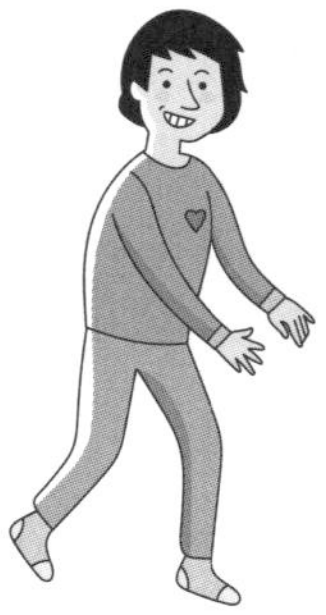

1 back ....
2 heart ....
3 ear ....
4 body ....
H 5 tooth ....
H 6 stomach ....

a	das Ohr	**d**	das Herz
b	der Rücken	**e**	der Bauch
c	der Körper	**f**	der Zahn

2 Complete these sentences with the correct German words from the box.

Arm Bein Finger Mund Hand Fuß Muskeln Haut Augen Nase Schulter

1 Ich habe Schmerzen in den ...., im .... und im .... (*muscles, leg, foot*)

2 Im Gesicht sind der .... und die .... (*mouth, eyes*)

H 3 Ich kann meinen .... und meine .... nicht bewegen. (*arm, shoulder*)

H 4 Herr Doktor, es geht mir nicht gut. Ich habe mir die .... und die .... verletzt. (*skin, nose*)

H 5 Zunächst konnte ich weder meine .... noch meinen .... spüren. (*hand, finger*)

G

Modal verbs in the **imperfect tense** have these endings. Note that there is no umlaut on modal verbs in the imperfect tense.

	können (*can, be able to*)	**dürfen** (*may, be allowed to*)	**müssen** (*must, have to*)	**wollen** (*want*)
ich	konn**te**	durf**te**	muss**te**	woll**te**
du	konn**test**	durf**test**	muss**test**	woll**test**
er/sie/es/man	konn**te**	durf**te**	muss**te**	woll**te**

Ich ***konnte*** *(nicht) joggen.*	I could (not) jog.
Du ***durftest*** *(nicht) laufen.*	You were (not) allowed to run.
Sie ***musste*** *ins Krankenhaus gehen.*	She had to go to the hospital.
Er ***wollte*** *nicht zum Arzt gehen.*	He did not want to go to the doctor.
H *Wir* ***wollten*** *das Medikament nicht nehmen.*	We did not want to take the medicine.
H *Ihr* ***durftet*** *keinen Sport machen.*	You were not allowed to do sports.
H *Sie* ***konnten*** *nicht laufen.*	You (formal. sg/pl) / They could not run.

3 Circle the correct form of the modal verb to complete each sentence.

1 Ich habe mir vor einem Monat das Bein gebrochen und **musste** / **müssen** / **musstest** eine Woche zu Hause bleiben.

2 Er hatte vor einer Woche Augenschmerzen und **konntest** / **konnte** / **können** nur wenig schlafen.

3 Sie hatte vor zwei Tagen Ohrenschmerzen und **wollen** / **wolltest** / **wollte** nicht schwimmen.

4 Er hatte vor zwei Monaten eine Krankheit und **durfte** / **dürfen** / **durftest** nicht zur Arbeit gehen.

5 Du hattest vor zwei Tagen Kopfschmerzen und **musste** / **musstest** / **müssen** zu Hause bleiben.

4 Complete these sentences with the correct imperfect tense form of the modal verb in brackets. Then translate the verb into English.

1 Sie war gesund, aber sie .... keinen Fußball spielen. (*dürfen*) ....

2 Du bist vor drei Tagen gefallen und .... dich nicht bewegen. (*können*) ....

3 Der Fahrer .... vor zwei Tagen ins Krankenhaus gehen. (*müssen*) ....

H 4 Der Unfall ist vor zwei Tagen passiert, aber ich .... nicht zum Arzt gehen. (*wollen*) ....

H 5 Es ist vor drei Tagen geschehen: Ich habe mir die Haut verletzt und .... das Blut nicht sehen. (*können*) ....

H 5 Fill in the missing imperfect tense modal verb in each sentence. Then write down on a separate sheet the English translation of the verb you added.

1 Der Patient hatte seit einer Woche Ohrenschmerzen und .... nicht einschlafen. (*can, be able to*)

2 Ich habe mir vor einer Woche beim Tennisspielen das Knie verletzt und .... mir beim Arzt einen Termin holen, um mich medizinisch untersuchen zu lassen. (*must, have to*)

3 Er hatte eine Krankheit und .... daher zwei Tage lang nicht in die Schule gehen. (*may, be allowed to*)

4 Sie hatte vor zwei Tagen beim Essen Bauchschmerzen, aber sie .... immer mehr essen. (*want*)

5 Du hast dir vor einem Monat beim Training den Fuß gebrochen und .... vorsichtig gehen. (*must, have to*)

> **H** Use ***beim*** + noun to say 'while doing something'.
> You can change any verb into a neuter noun simply by giving it a capital letter:
> *Ich habe mir **beim** Joggen das Bein verletzt.*
> I injured my leg **while** jogging.

F 6 Translate these sentences into English on a separate sheet.

1 Ich habe Rückenschmerzen und ich kann nichts machen.

2 Ich habe mir vor zwei Monaten die Hand gebrochen.

3 Ich will Tennis spielen, aber ich habe Armschmerzen.

4 Vor zwei Tagen hat mein Bruder gefragt, „Was ist los?“

5 Ich hatte vor sechs Tagen Fußschmerzen und ich konnte nicht springen.

> ***vor*** means **ago** and ***seit*** means **since/for**. They both take the dative case:
> ***vor*** *ei**nem** Monat* one month ago
> ***seit*** *ei**ner** Woche* for a week

H 7 Translate these sentences into German on a separate sheet.

1 Two years ago, I broke my hand while climbing.

2 I had to go to hospital in Cologne.

3 I wanted to do sport again immediately, but I wasn't allowed to.

4 I had to stay at home for four weeks.

5 Now I am well and I can begin activities again.

3 Was möchte ich verbessern?

- Revising present, past and future tenses
- H Using infinitive constructions with *zu*

1 Draw lines to match up the English infinitives (1–7) with their German translations (a–g). Then draw lines to match up the German infinitives with their past participles (i–vii).

1 to sit	**a** schlagen	**i** aufgegeben
2 to hit	**b** essen	**ii** reduziert
3 to eat	**c** fernsehen	**iii** gegessen
4 to watch television	**d** sitzen	**iv** ferngesehen
H **5** to give up	**e** reduzieren	**v** geschlagen
H **6** to decide	**f** beschließen	**vi** gesessen
H **7** to reduce	**g** aufgeben	**vii** beschlossen

G

Remember that the **perfect tense** (a past tense) is formed with ***haben*** or ***sein*** + past participle. Some past participles are irregular. The **future tense** is formed with ***werden*** + infinitive.

infinitive	**present tense**	**perfect tense**	**future tense**
sein (*to be*)	ich bin	ich bin ... gewesen	ich werde ... sein
schlafen (*to sleep*)	du schläfst	du hast ... geschlafen	du wirst ... schlafen
verändern (*to change, alter*)	er/sie/es/man verändert	er/sie/es/man ... hat verändert	er/sie/es/man wird ... verändern
gehen (*to go, walk*)	wir gehen	wird **sind** ... gegangen	wir werden ... gehen
bringen (*to bring*)	ihr bringt	ihr habt ... gebracht	ihr werdet ... bringen
machen (*to make, do*)	sie machen	sie haben ... gemacht	sie werden ... machen

2 Draw lines to match up the problems with the solutions.

1. Ich habe nicht genug geschlafen.
2. Mein Hund isst zu viel und ist zu dick.
3. Ich bin nicht aktiv und ich habe Rückenschmerzen.
4. Ich habe Augenschmerzen.
5. Ich trinke nicht genug.
6. Ich habe mir die Hand verletzt.

a Ich werde mehr Wasser trinken.
b Ich werde mehr Sport treiben.
c Er wird sich mehr bewegen.
d Ich werde früher ins Bett gehen.
e Ich werde mein Handy weniger benutzen.
f Ich werde den Ball nicht so stark schlagen.

3 Rewrite these sentences in the perfect tense.

1. Ich esse zu viel Fastfood. ....
2. Ich benutze mein Handy weniger. ....
3. Ich bewege mich mehr. ....
4. Ich rauche weniger. ....
5. Ich werde weniger Zeit auf dem Handy verbringen.

....

G

H Some verbs require the addition of ***zu*** before the infinitive. As with ***um ... zu***, you need to use a comma before the infinitive construction:
*Ich beginne, mehr Obst **zu** essen.* I begin / am beginning to eat more fruit.
Ich beschließe/entscheide/habe vor/plane/versuche/verspreche, ... zu ...
I decide/intend/plan/plan/try/promise to ...
Modal verbs do not follow this pattern and do **not need *zu*** before the infinitive:
*Ich **muss** mehr Obst essen.*

H 4 Complete these sentences with a word from the box. You may need to change the form of the verb according to the tense needed: present, past or future.

aufgeben treiben erhöhen essen sein reduzieren

1 Ich habe begonnen, mehr Sport zu ...., und das ist eine gute Methode, um gesünder zu sein.
2 Ich werde das Problem lösen und bald wieder in Form ....
3 Ich verspreche, ich werde es schaffen, mehr Obst und Gemüse dazu zu ....
4 Ich habe eine Veränderung gebraucht und mich gut verhalten, denn ich habe die Zeit auf meinem Handy ....
5 Ein Punkt ist: Meine Ernährung ist nicht so gut, aber ich habe zumindest Fastfood vollständig ....
6 Mein neues Konzept ist: Ich werde meine Zeit im Fitness-Studio ...., um mich mehr zu bewegen.

F 5 Translate these sentences into German.

1 I often have sore eyes. ....
2 Now I spend less time on my mobile phone.
....
3 Two weeks ago I ate too much fast food.
....
4 In the future I will watch less television.
....
5 I will also do more sport and be more active.
....

H 6 Translate these sentences into English.

1 Ich kann mich nicht konzentrieren, weil ich zu müde bin.
....
2 Aber ich plane, das nächste Woche zu ändern!
....
3 Ich werde versuchen, täglich früher ins Bett zu gehen.
....
4 Ich habe es schon geschafft, die Zeit vor dem Fernsehen zu reduzieren!
....
5 In der Zukunft werde ich mich auch mehr bewegen und gesünder essen.
....

4 Gute Tage, schlechte Tage

F Using *wenn*

1 Underline the verbs in each sentence and write down their infinitive forms.

1 Ich weine, weil ich traurig bin. ....

2 Ich mache Sport, weil ich wenig Energie habe. ....

3 Ich bleibe zu Hause, weil das Wetter schlecht ist. ....

4 Ich höre klassische Musik, weil sie spannend ist. ....

5 Ich spreche mit meinen Eltern, weil ich Schwierigkeiten in der Schule habe. ....

2 Separate out the words and write out the sentences on a separate sheet. Insert the comma in the correct place.

1 WenndasWetterschlechtistliestsieeinBuch.

2 WennichtraurigbinsprecheichmitmeinerSchwester.

3 WennichkeineEnergiehabemacheichzweiStundenSport.

4 WennichmichalleinfühlerufeichmeineFreundean.

5 WennesmirnichtgutgehtbleibeichimBett.

6 WennicheineschwierigeWochehabegeheichspazieren.

G

The conjunction ***wenn*** can mean 'when', 'whenever' or 'if', and is used to express what you do in certain situations. Note the **verb–comma–verb** structure:

Wenn *ich nicht glücklich* ***bin, sprechen*** *ich mit Freunden.*

When I **am** not happy, I **talk** to friends.

3 Rewrite each sentence, putting the words into the correct order.

1 das / ich / Wetter / ist, / wandern. / gern / Wenn / schön / gehe

....

2 meiner / gibt, / spreche / mit / Wenn es / Lehrerin. / Probleme / ich

....

3 habe, / Geld / ins / Wenn / gehe / genug / ich / Kino. / ich

....

4 schlafe, / glücklich. / bin / gut / ich / ich / Wenn

....

5 Wenn / geht / meine / ich / treffe, / es / besser. / Freunde / mir

....

- Each sentence starts with *Wenn*.
- Look for the words with a comma or full stop to help you organise the sentences. Remember, verb–comma–verb.

4 Translate these sentences into German on a separate sheet.

1 When I use my mobile phone less, I sleep better.

2 Whenever I'm too thin, I eat more.

3 If I have a headache, I go to the doctor.

4 When I don't feel well, I see a funny film.

5 Whenever I speak to my friends, I am happy.

4 Gute Tage, schlechte Tage

- **H** Using *wenn*
- **H** Using set phrases with *zu*

H 1 Complete each sentence using a word from the box.

stolz erkennen enthalten sinnvoll körperliche

1 Es ist ...., über Probleme zu sprechen.

2 Im Gegensatz dazu ist Bewegung gut für die .... Gesundheit.

3 Du kannst .... auf dich sein, denn du hast die Hoffnung nicht aufgegeben.

4 Wir müssen ...., dass negativ sein nicht gut für uns ist.

5 Nur Fastfood essen reicht nicht für eine gute Ernährung – jedes Gericht soll Gemüse ...., weil das gesund ist.

H 2 Complete each sentence using a verb from the box.

wäre wäre würde würde hätte

1 Wenn ich aktiver wäre, ... ich mich besser fühlen.

2 Wenn ich nicht so oft traurig ...., würde ich mich nicht verstecken, sondern mehr lachen.

3 Wenn ich mehr Zeit für Sport hätte, ... ich nicht so oft Rückenschmerzen kriegen.

4 Wenn ich positiver wäre, ... ich mehr Hoffnung und mir würde alles gelingen.

5 Wenn ich ein Haustier hätte, würde mir das Freude bringen und das .... entspannend.

G

H The conjunction ***wenn*** is often used together with the imperfect subjunctive (***hätte, wäre***) and **conditional** (***würde***) to express what you **would** do **if** you **had ...** or **if** you **were ...**

Wenn ich mehr Zeit ***hätte, würde*** *ich mehr lesen.*

If I **had** more time, I **would** read more.

Wenn ich weniger traurig ***wäre, würde*** *ich mehr lachen.*

If I **were** less sad, I **would** laugh more.

Note the **verb–comma–verb** structure and the infinitive at the end of the sentence.

Wenn also means '**when**' and can be used with the present tense.

Wenn *das Wetter gut ist, gehe ich spazieren.*

When the weather is good, I go for a walk.

H 3 Draw lines to match up the sentence halves.

1 Wenn ich Gesundheitsprobleme hätte,

2 Wenn ich müde wäre,

3 Wenn ich allein und traurig wäre,

4 Wenn ich weniger Druck hätte,

a würde ich mit meinen engsten Geschwistern darüber sprechen.

b würde ich mich besser entspannen können.

c würde ich mit meinem Doktor einen Termin machen.

d würde ich versuchen, früher ins Bett zu gehen.

H 4 Translate these sentences into German on a separate sheet.

1 It is really important for physical health to do sport.

2 If there are problems, it's useful to talk about them with friends.

3 If I didn't have a best friend, I would be very sad.

4 Of course, it is also necessary to be active and to exercise.

5 If I had more time, I would go to the gym every day.

H ***zu*** + infinitive is used after some adjectives:

Es ist wichtig, positiv zu sein.

It is important to be positive.

Es ist sinnvoll, (useful) / *nötig,* (necessary) / *schwierig,* (difficult) ...

Put a comma before the ***zu*** phrase.

5 Das finde ich wichtig!

Understanding questions in different tenses

1 Draw lines to match up the questions with the answers.

1 Machst du Sport?
2 Isst du gesund?
3 Ist eine Karriere wichtig für dich?
H **4** Bist du erfolgreich?
H **5** Was ist wichtig für dich?

a Ja, ich esse viel Obst und Gemüse.
b Ja, aber meine Gesundheit ist mir wichtiger.
c Ja, ich spiele in einer Mannschaft Fußball.
d Persönliche Werte und eine gute Karriere.
e Ja, aber ich habe auch viel Druck.

2 Unjumble the letters to rewrite the words correctly. Add the definite article (*der*, *die*, or *das*). Then write the English translation next to each word.

1 uLnae ....
2 scanhMnaft ....
3 aKrrriee ....
4 ndesuehGit ....
H **5** Snin ....
H **6** rWte ....

G

Remember:
Use the **present tense** to talk about what you **do** or **are doing now**:
Isst *du Obst?* **Do** you **eat** fruit? / **Are** you **eating** fruit?
Use the **perfect** and **imperfect tense** to talk about something that happened in the **past**:
Hast *du Obst* ***gegessen****?* Did you **eat** fruit?
Hattest *du Obst?* **Did** you **have** fruit?
Use the **future** tense to talk about something that will happen in the **future**:
Wirst *du Obst* ***essen****?* **Will** you **eat** fruit?

3 Underline the verb(s) in each question. Then write which tense each question is in: past, present or future.

1 Was machst du, wenn du Probleme hast? ....
2 Wirst du weniger fernsehen? ....
3 Warst du im Vergleich zu heute früher aktiver? ....
4 Wann hast du zum letzten Mal ein Buch gelesen? ....
5 Lebst du normalerweise gesund? ....
6 Was hast du gemacht, wenn du traurig warst? ....
7 Was wirst du nach der Schule machen? ....
H **8** Wie erhalten Sie Ihre Gesundheit? ....

4 Complete these German questions and their English translations.

1 .... nach der Schule machen?

What will you ....*?*

2 Ist Tieren helfen ....?

.... *important to you?*

3 ...., wenn du krank warst?

What did you do ....*?*

4 .... einen Wettbewerb haben?

Will you ....*?*

H 5 .... mit dem Erfolg gestiegen?

Has the pressure ....*?*

H 5 Draw lines to match up the questions with the answers.

1 Sind Wettbewerbe spannend für dich?

2 Wirst du nach der Schule an die Universität gehen?

3 Warum wirst du dir eine Arbeit suchen?

4 Was hast du mit dem Geld von Opa gemacht?

5 Wirst du Sportschuhe mitnehmen?

6 Was hat deine Familie dazu gesagt?

a Ja, falls ich wandern gehe.

b Meine Mutter begann, zu weinen. Meine Schwester dagegen hat die Idee gut gefunden.

c Nein, ich werde mir eine interessante Arbeit suchen, um Lernen und Geldverdienen zu verbinden.

d Ich beobachte gern Tiere und habe mir eine Kamera gekauft.

e Ja, allerdings finde ich Training genauso spannend.

f Ich werde reisen und ich brauche Geld dafür.

F 6 Translate these sentences into English.

1 Was hast du in letzter Zeit für deine Familie gemacht? ....

2 Wie wichtig ist dir die Schule? ....

3 Möchtest du dir eine Stelle suchen? ....

4 Wirst du in der Zukunft mehr Sport machen? ....

5 Bist du gestern joggen gegangen? ....

H 7 Translate these sentences into German on a separate sheet.

1 What is important to me in life today?

2 Success and a career were the most important things for me in the past.

3 But now I find that teamwork is very meaningful.

4 I notice that it is always important to have good health.

5 In the future, I will eat more healthily and do more sport.

Glossary

bold = this word will appear in Higher exams only

Alkohol (m)	alcohol
allerdings	though, indeed, certainly
am höchsten	(the) highest (post-noun)
am meisten	(the) most (post-noun)
am nächsten	(the) next, nearest (post-noun)
Arm (m)	arm
auch	also, too, as well
aufgeben	(to) give up, quit
aufpassen	(to) pay attention, take care
Auge (nt)	eye
bald	soon
Ball (m)	ball
Bauch (m)	belly
begann	(I, she, he, it) began, started
(aux)...begonnen	began, started / (have, has) begun, started (pp)
Bein (nt)	leg
bemerken	(to) notice
beobachten	(to) observe, watch
beschließen	(to) decide
besser	better
bestellen	(to) order, reserve | ordering, reserving
betrunken	drunk
bewegen; sich acc. bewegen	(to) move | moving; (to) exercise; exercising
Bewegung (f)	movement, motion, exercise
Bier (nt)	beer
Blut (nt)	blood

brechen	(to) break | breaking
Brot (nt)	bread
Cola (f)	cola
dafür	for it/that/them, **for it**, **for that**
dagegen	on the other hand, **against it**
daher	from there, therefore
das geht	that's fine, that's possible
dazu	in addition, furthermore, besides
dazu	to that, for that, in addition, furthermore
der/die/das beste	the best (pre-noun)
der/die/das höchste	the highest (pre-noun)
der/die/das meiste	the most (pre-noun)
der/die/das nächste	the next, nearest (pre-noun)
dick	fat
Doktor, Dr. (m)	doctor
Droge (f)	drug
Druck (m)	pressure, stress
dünn	thin
durfte	(I, she, it, one) was allowed to
durftest	(you (sing informal)) were allowed to
Durst (m)	thirst
Ei (nt)	egg
einschlafen	(to) fall asleep, doze off
Eis (nt)	ice, ice cream
Energie (f)	energy
enthalten	(to) contain
entspannend	relaxing

erhalten	*(to) receive, preserve, maintain*
erhöhen	*(to) raise, increase*
erkennen	*(to) recognise, admit, realise*
Ernährung (f)	*food, diet, nutrition*
es geht mir gut/ schlecht	*I am fine, well / not well*
Essen (nt)	*food, meal*
Fahrer (m)	*driver*
fallen	*(to) fall, decrease | falling, decreasing*
falls	*in case, if*
Fastfood (nt)	*fast food*
Finger (m)	*finger*
Fitness (f)	*fitness*
Fitness-Studio (nt)	*gym*
Freude (f)	*joy, pleasure*
früher	*previously, in former times, in the past*
fühlen	*(to) feel | feeling*
Fuß (m)	*foot*
(aux)...gebracht	*brought / (have, has) brought (pp)*
(aux)...gebrochen	*broken*
Gegensatz (m)	*opposite, contrast*
gehören	*(to) belong | belonging*
gelingen	*(to) succeed | succeeding*
Gemüse (nt)	*vegetables*
genauso	*just as*
Gericht (nt)	*dish*
geschehen	*(to) happen, occur, take place*
Gesicht (nt)	*face*
gesund	*healthy, healthily*
Gesundheit (f)	*health*
Hähnchen (nt)	*chicken*
Hand (f)	*hand*
hätte	*(I, she, he, it) had / would have*
Haut (f)	*skin*
helfen	*(to) help | helping*
Herr (m)	*Mr., Lord (addressing God)*
Herz (nt)	*heart*
Hoffnung (f)	*hope*
höher	*higher, taller*
Hunger (m)	*hunger*
in Form sein	*(to) be in form, be in good shape | being in form, being in good shape*
in letzter Zeit	*recently, lately*
ist	*(she, he, it, one) is / is being*
jetzt	*now, currently*
joggen	*(to) jog | jogging*
Kaffee (m)	*coffee*
Karriere (f)	*career*
Käse (m)	*cheese*
kaum	*hardly*
klettern	*(to) climb*
Knie (nt) (pl)	*knee, knees*
konnte	*(I, she, he, it, one) was able to, could*
konntest	*(you (sing informal)) were able to, could*
konzentrieren (auf acc. + noun)	*(to) concentrate (on + noun)*
Konzept (nt)	*concept, idea, plan*
Kopf (m)	*head*
Körper (m)	*body*
körperlich	*physical, physically*
Krankenhaus (nt)	*hospital*

		😐	🙂	😎
Krankheit (f)	*illness, disease*			
kriegen	*(to) get, receive | getting, receiving*			
Lauf (m)	*course, run, race*			
Leistung (f)	*performance, achievement*			
los	*rid of, going on*			
lösen	*(to) solve, loosen | solving, loosening*			
Mannschaft (f)	*team*			
Medikament (nt)	*medicine*			
medizinisch	*medical*			
mehr	*more*			
Methode (f)	*method, technique*			
Milch (f)	*milk*			
mindestens	*at least, minimum*			
Monat (m)	*month*			
müde	*tired*			
Mund (m)	*mouth*			
Muskel (m)	*muscle*			
musste	*(I, she, he, it, one) had to*			
musstest	*(you (sing informal)) had to*			
Nase (f)	*nose*			
negativ	*negative*			
nehmen	*(to) take, have something to eat or drink | taking, having something to eat or drink*			
Obst (nt)	*fruit*			
Ohr (nt)	*ear*			
passieren	*(to) take place, happen, occur | taking place, happening, occurring*			
Patient (m)	*patient*			
Person (f)	*person*			
persönlich	*personal*			
positiv	*positive*			
Protein (nt)	*protein*			
Punkt (m)	*dot, point, full stop*			
rauchen	*(to) smoke | smoking*			
Raum (m)	*room, space*			
reduzieren	*(to) reduce, decrease*			
regelmäßig	*regular, regularly*			
reichen	*(to) reach, be enough*			
relativ	*relative, relatively, comparatively*			
Restaurant (nt)	*restaurant*			
Rücken (m)	*back*			
Runde (f)	*round, lap (sport)*			
schaffen	*(to) create, manage, accomplish*			
scharf	*sharp, spicy, hot*			
schlagen	*(to) hit, beat | hitting, beating*			
schlank	*slim, thin*			
Schmerz (m)	*pain, ache*			
Schmerzen (pl)	*pains, aches*			
Schulter (f)	*shoulder*			
schwach	*weak*			
Schweizer (adj)	*Swiss*			
Schwierigkeit (f)	*difficulty*			
seit	*since, for*			
sich acc. verhalten	*(to) behave, act*			
sich entspannen	*(to) relax, chill out*			
Sinn (m)	*sense, meaning*			
sinnvoll	*sensible, meaningful, wise*			
sitzen	*(to) sit | sitting*			
so…wie	*as…as*			
sofort	*immediately*			
sondern	*(but) rather*			

springen	*(to) jump | jumping*
spüren	*(to) sense, notice, feel*
stark	*strong*
steigen	*(to) increase, go up, climb | increasing, going up, climbing*
stolz	*proud*
Stunde (f)	*hour, lesson, period (school timetable)*
süchtig	*addicted, hooked on*
telefonieren	*(to) (make a telephone) call*
Termin (m)	*appointment, date, meeting*
Tisch (m)	*table*
Trainer (m)	*coach*
Training (nt)	*training*
treiben	*(to) do (sport), drive, pursue | doing (sport), driving, pursuing*
übergewichtig	*overweight*
um...zu (+ infinitive)	*in order to (+ verb)*
und so weiter, usw.	*and so on, etc.*
Unfall (m)	*accident, crash*
untersuchen	*(to) examine, investigate, research*
Veränderung (f)	*change*
verbinden; sich acc. verbinden	*(to) connect, link, unite*
Vergleich (m)	*comparison*
verletzen	*(to) injure, hurt | injuring, hurting*
versprechen	*(to) promise | promising*
verstecken	*(to) hide*
verzichten auf acc. + noun	*(to) do without + noun*
vollständig	*complete, completely, thoroughly*
vorsichtig	*cautious, careful, wary*
wählen	*(to) choose, elect, vote, select | choosing, electing, voting, selecting*
wäre	*(I, she, he, it) were / would be*
Wasser (nt)	*water*
Wein (m)	*wine*
weinen	*(to) cry | crying*
wenig	*little*
wenn	*if, when, whenever*
Wert (m)	*value, worth*
Wettbewerb (m)	*competition, contest*
wollte	*(I, she, he, it, one) wanted (to)*
Wurst (f)	*sausage*
Zahl (f)	*number*
zahlen	*(to) pay | paying*
Zahn (m)	*tooth*
Zigarette (f)	*cigarette*
Zucker (m)	*sugar*
zum Beispiel, z.B.	*for example, e.g.*
zumindest	*at least*
zunächst	*first, at first, to begin with, for now, for the time being*
Zusammen-arbeit (f)	*cooperation, teamwork*

Kulturzone Wo spricht man Deutsch?

- Revising the comparative
- H Revising the superlative

1 Draw lines to match up the German with the English nouns.

1 die Größe	**a** height
2 die Höhe	**b** country
3 das Land	**c** language
4 der Meter	**d** size
5 die Sprache	**e** location
H **6** der König	**f** metre
H **7** die Lage	**g** report
H **8** der Bericht	**h** king

2 Complete each German sentence using an adjective from the box.

beliebt freundlich grün hoch kalt klein lang niedrig

1 Wissen Sie, dass der Berg sehr .... ist?	*Do you know that the mountain is very high?*
2 Du weißt, dass das Wetter meist .... ist.	*You know that the weather is mostly cold.*
3 Der nationale Fluss ist sehr	*The national river is very long.*
4 Die Stadt ist zu	*The town is too small.*
H **5** Die Lage ist ziemlich	*The location is quite green.*
H **6** Die Bevölkerung ist	*The population is low.*
H **7** Die Einwohner sind	*The inhabitants are friendly.*
H **8** Die Altstadt ist bei der Öffentlichkeit	*The old town is popular with the public.*

3 Complete these sentences with the correct comparative form of the verb in brackets. Then translate the comparative adjectives into English on a separate sheet.

1 Der Fluss ist zwanzig Zentimeter .... als der Rhein. (*lang*)

2 Das Wetter ist .... als in Deutschland. (*kalt*)

3 Die Stadt ist .... als Bern. (*groß*)

4 Jemand ist .... als der Junge. (*alt*)

5 Das Mädchen ist .... als die Frau. (*klein*)

6 Die Berge sind .... als in Österreich. (*hoch*)

7 Die linke Straße ist viel .... als die rechte Straße. (*eng*)

G

Use the **comparative** to compare things, people and places.

To form the comparative, add **-er** to the end of the adjective and use *als* to say 'than'.

klein → *klein**er***

*Der Garten ist **kleiner als** das Feld.* The garden is **smaller than** the field.

Some adjectives add an umlaut to the vowel in the comparative:

groß → *gr**ö**ß**er***

*Der Erwachsene ist **größer als** das Kind.* The adult is **bigger than** the child.

You need to know how to form large numbers in German.
500 – fünfhundert 1000 – (ein)tausend
5000 – fünftausend 2015 – zweitausendfünfzehn
39 678 – neununddreißigtausendsechshundertachtundsiebzig
German uses small spaces or a full stop to separate thousands and a comma as a decimal point – the opposite of the format used in English!

4 Write out these numbers in words in German.

1 550 ....
2 398 ....
3 2 025 ....
4 4 635 ....
5 1 997 ....
6 41 285 ....

H 5 Complete these sentences with the correct superlative form of the adjective in brackets. Then translate the superlative adjectives into English on a separate sheet.

1 Das ist das .... Schloss. (*groß*)
2 Bern ist die .... Hauptstadt. (*alt*)
3 Die Donau ist der .... Fluss. (*lang*)
4 Das Matterhorn ist der .... Berg. (*hoch*)
5 Luxemburg hat die .... Bevölkerung. (*niedrig*)
6 Liechtenstein ist das .... Land. (*klein*)

G

H Use the **superlative** form of an adjective to describe something as 'the most' or 'the least'. To form the superlative, add ***-(e)ste*** to the adjective.
Some adjectives also add an umlaut to the vowel.
The adjective needs to agree with the noun it is describing.
hoch: *der h**ö**ch**ste** Punkt*
the highest point
alt: *das **ä**lt**este** Schloss*
the oldest castle

F 6 Translate these sentences into German.

1 I live in Austria. ....
2 A lot of people live in Berlin. ....
3 The national day is in October. ....
4 Vienna is bigger than Cologne. ....
5 In the winter it is colder than in Germany. ....
....

H 7 Translate these sentences into English on a separate sheet.

1 Ich lebe in der Schweiz und die meisten Leute wohnen in Zürich.
2 Die Hauptstadt ist Bern und Bern ist kleiner als Zürich.
3 Der längste Fluss ist 292 km lang und er geht durch die Stadtmitte.
4 Ich besuche zweimal pro Jahr das Schloss.
5 Der Nationalfeiertag ist am ersten August und wir feiern mit der Familie.

1 Wo wohnst du?

- Using prepositions followed by the dative
- Using a variety of adjectives with intensifiers and qualifiers

1 **Choose the correct English translation by selecting a word from the wall. There are more words on the wall than you need.**

mosque	bridge	church	airport	castle
station	synagogue	bank	stadium	temple

1 der Bahnhof ....

2 die Brücke ....

3 der Flughafen ....

4 die Kirche ....

5 die Moschee ....

6 das Stadion ....

7 die Synagoge ....

8 der Tempel ....

2 **Circle the correct adjective to complete each English translation.**

1 Das Dorf ist sehr sauber. *The village is very **new** / **clean**.*

2 Die Stadt ist nicht schmutzig. *The town isn't **dirty** / **quiet**.*

3 Die Gegend ist ziemlich sicher. *The area is quite **safe** / **quiet**.*

4 Die Stadtmitte ist echt alt. *The town centre is really **old** / **loud**.*

H **5** Die Umgebung ist ganz angenehm. *The surroundings are quite **cultural** / **pleasant**.*

H **6** Der Bereich ist echt grün. *The area is really **modern** / **green**.*

3 **Complete these sentences by translating the words in brackets into German.**

1 Die Landschaft ist .... (*quite green*).

2 Das Gebiet ist .... (*really quiet*).

3 Der Ort ist .... (*quite narrow*).

4 Das einzige Geschäft ist .... (*really new*).

5 Der Verkehr ist ein .... (*very big problem*).

H **6** Ich habe keine Ahnung. Ich denke, dass der Bau .... (*quite old*) ist.

> **G** Use **intensifiers** or **qualifiers** which make an adjective weaker or stronger.
>
> ***ziemlich*** *frisch* quite fresh
> ***ganz*** *jung* quite young
> ***echt*** *eng* really narrow
> ***sehr*** *breit* very wide

4 **Read the grammar box on the next page. Complete these German sentences with the correct article.**

1 Ich komme aus .... Dorf (*nt*). *I come from a village.*

2 Die Straße zu .... Schule (*f*) ist sehr breit. *The street to the school is very wide.*

3 Die Fahrt von .... Brücke (*f*) her ist kurz. *The trip here from the bridge is short.*

4 Die Universität liegt bei .... Fluss (*m*). *The university is situated by a river.*

5 Ich gehe mit .... Familie (*f*). *I go with my family.*

6 Das Museum ist gegenüber .... Geschäft (*nt*). *The museum is opposite the shop.*

G

Some **prepositions** are **always** followed by the **dative**.

ab from (with time expressions)
aus out of, from
außer except for
bei at, near
gegenüber opposite
mit with
nach after, to
seit since
von from
zu to

*Ich wohne **mit meiner** Großmutter.*
I live with my grandmother.
*Ich komme **aus der** Stadt.* I come from the town.
*Ich lebe **bei einem** Fluss.* I live by a river.
*Die Schule liegt **gegenüber dem** Schloss.*
The school is opposite the castle.

Some prepositions are shortened when used before *dem/der*: *bei dem* ⟶ *beim*, *von dem* ⟶ *vom*, *zu dem* ⟶ *zum*, *zu der* ⟶ *zur*

	masculine	**feminine**	**neuter**	**plural**
definite article: 'the'	dem	der	dem	den
indefinite article: 'a', 'an' **negatives** **possessive adjectives**	einem keinem meinem	einer keiner meiner	einem keinem meinem	– keinen meinen

5 Circle the correct article to complete each sentence. Then translate the sentences into English.

1 Es gibt **keinen / kein / keine** Kino (*nt*). ....

2 Es gibt **einen / ein / eine** Schule (*f*). ....

3 Das passt nicht – es gibt **keinen / kein / keine** Bahnhof (*m*). ....

....

4 Es gab **einen / ein / eine** Theater (*nt*). ....

5 Es gab **keinen / kein / keine** Universität (*f*). ....

G

Es gibt is always followed by the accusative.
*Es gibt **einen** Flughafen.* There's an airport.
*Es gibt **keine** Bank.* There's no bank.
*Es gibt **ein** Geschäft.* There's a shop.
*Es gibt **viele** Kosten.* There are many costs.

F 6 Translate these sentences into English.

1 Ich wohne in einem sehr kleinen Dorf. ....

2 Lebst du mit deiner Familie? ....

3 Es gibt keinen Bahnhof. ....

4 Im Süden gibt es eine Post und einige Geschäfte.

....

5 Es gibt nichts für Jugendliche, aber das Museum ist jeden Tag offen.

....

H 7 Translate these sentences into German on a separate sheet.

1 My town is in the east of Germany.

2 I live on the edge of the town.

3 There is no cinema but there is a castle opposite the school.

4 There was a theatre, but it is closed now.

5 The area is very cultural but quite ugly.

2 Wie fährst du?

- Using prepositions with the accusative
- Using correct word order

1 Match up the German words with the types of transport. Write the correct letter.

1 das Fahrrad ....
2 das Auto ....
3 der Zug ....
4 das Schiff ....
5 das Flugzeug ....
6 der Bus ....
H 7 die U-Bahn ....
H 8 die Straßenbahn ....

a

b

c

d

e

f
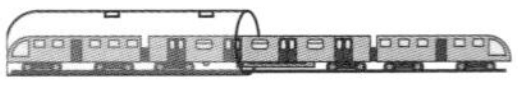
g

h

2 Draw lines to match up the sentence halves.

1 Die Reise dauert
2 Ich komme mit
3 Ich reise
4 Die Schule ist
5 Die Bahn ist schneller
6 Ich fahre mit den
7 Ich fliege mit dem

a als das Fahrrad.
b öffentlichen Bussen.
c Flugzeug.
d dem Auto nach Hause.
e mit einem privaten Bus.
f zwei Stunden.
g ganz nah.

Try to work out the meaning of German sentences as you work through exercises. Don't be disheartened if you see words you don't know yet! Use the glossary at the end of the module to help you.

G

Some **prepositions** are **always** followed by the **accusative**.

bis until, up to
durch through
für for
gegen against
ohne without
um around, round
H *entlang* along (goes after the noun)

*Die Bahn geht **durch die** Stadt.*
The railway goes through the town.

*Ich kaufe ein Geschenk **für meinen** Vater.*
I buy a present for my dad.

The **masculine** articles change in the accusative:

	the	**a/an**
nominative	der	ein
accusative	de**n**	ein**en**

3 Complete these German sentences with the correct preposition and article.

1 I put the picture against the wall. — *Ich stelle das Bild* .... *Wand (f).*
2 I apologise that I don't have a present for my brother. — *Ich entschuldige mich, dass ich kein Geschenk* .... *Bruder (m) habe.*
3 Why are you driving through the town centre? — *Warum fährst du* .... *Stadtmitte (f)?*
4 She drives without her dad. — *Sie fährt* .... *Vater (m).*
H 5 I drive along the street. — *Ich fahre* .... *Straße (f)* ....
H 6 He leads the horses through the village. — *Er führt die Pferde* .... *Dorf (nt).*

G

Remember these key word order rules:
- First comes **time**, then **manner**, then **place**.
- The verb is always the second idea of the sentence.
- A modal verb sends the second verb (the infinitive) to the end of the clause.
- Some conjunctions such as ***weil*** (because) and ***obwohl*** (although) send the verb to the end of the clause:

*Ich fahre gern mit dem Zug, **obwohl** das teuer **ist**.*
I like travelling by train, although it's expensive.

4 Rearrange the words to create correct sentences.

1 Nächstes Wochenende mit dem Flugzeug in die Ferien fliegen wir

....

2 Die Fahrt dauern, eine Stunde kann weil nicht in der Nähe das ist

....

3 nach Deutschland Ich darf machen eine Reise

....

4 Entschuldigung, den Bus erreichen ich muss

....

H 5 Sie nach Hause, immer fährt mit dem Auto weil fern das ist

....

H 6 mit der Straßenbahn Ich jeden Tag in die Schule, fahre weil gute Verbindungen man hat

....

H 5 Join the sentences using the conjunction in brackets. Remember to change the word order in the subordinate clause. Write on a separate sheet.

1 Ihr fahrt oft mit dem Zug. Das ist sehr schnell. (*weil*)

2 Sie fährt nicht gern mit dem Bus. Das kann billig sein. (*obwohl*)

3 Ich fahre lieber mit einem Fahrzeug. Die Schule ist weit entfernt. (*weil*)

4 Sie reisen gar nicht gern mit dem Boot. Das kann praktisch sein. (*obwohl*)

5 Ich muss den Bus erreichen. Ich will nicht spät ankommen. (*weil*)

F 6 Translate these sentences into German on a separate sheet.

1 I like travelling by bike.

2 I like going on foot, although it's slow.

3 We like going by bus because it's cheap.

4 The journey can last an hour.

5 He drove through the town.

H 7 Translate these sentences into English on a separate sheet.

1 Ich nehme oft das Fahrrad mit, weil das praktisch ist.

2 Wenn ich in die Ferien fahre, reise ich lieber mit dem Boot, obwohl das langsam ist.

3 Es kommt auf die Geschwindigkeit an, aber man kann viele Sachen vom Auto sehen.

4 Wir fahren mit der Straßenbahn durch die Stadt, weil das am schnellsten ist.

5 Man muss mit den öffentlichen Bussen fahren, aber sie sind sehr schmutzig.

3 Wo gehst du gern einkaufen?

- Using compound nouns and plurals of nouns
- H Using dual-case prepositions followed by the dative

1 Unjumble the letters to find the German verbs. Then translate them into English.

1 evrukeanf ....
2 stenok ....
3 cksicneh ....
4 ienakfune ....
5 psrena ....
6 ebomkemn ....

2 Work out the meanings of these compound nouns.

1 das Einkaufszentrum ....
2 die Handtasche ....
3 das Kleidungsgeschäft ....
4 der Supermarkt ....
5 das Schuhgeschäft ....
6 das Käsegeschäft ....
H 7 der Buchladen ....

G In German you can combine two or more words to make a new noun. These are known as **compound nouns**. Sometimes extra letters may be added to make pronunciation easier. It's useful to work out the meaning of each part of the compound noun as this helps to work out the meaning of the whole.

3 Complete these German translations with the correct plural noun.

1 Some supermarkets are very expensive.
Einige .... sind sehr teuer.

2 I like these bags.
Mir gefallen diese ....

3 You can easily find the prices.
Man kann einfach die .... finden.

4 You can send clothes directly back with the apps.
Man kann die Kleidung direkt mit den .... zurückschicken.

5 Some things arrive straight away.
Einige .... kommen sofort an.

H 6 Some products have very low costs.
Einige .... haben sehr niedrige Kosten.

G There are different ways of making nouns **plural** in German. You can follow patterns to work out how to form the plurals of different nouns.

	singular	**plural**
(-e)	Geschäft	Geschäft**e**
(¨e)	Supermarkt	Superm**ä**rkt**e**
(-n)	Straße	Straße**n**
(-en)	Uhr	Uhr**en**
(-)	Zimmer	Zimmer
(-er)	Kind	Kind**er**
(¨er)	Krankenhaus	Krankenh**ä**us**er**
(-s)	T-Shirt	T-Shirt**s**

F 4 Translate these sentences into English.

1 Ich kaufe sehr gern Taschen. ....

2 Ich bekomme die Kleidung direkt nach Hause. ....

3 Man soll online einkaufen, weil das einfach ist. ....

4 Die Preise waren sehr hoch. ....

5 Man kann die Sachen einfach zurückschicken. ....

H 5 Circle the correct article to complete each sentence. Then translate the sentences into English.

1 Ich habe die App auf **meinem** / **meiner** / **meinen** Handy (*nt*).

....

2 Über **dem** / **der** / **den** Kleidung (*f*) steht der Preis.

....

3 Das Einkaufszentrum liegt zwischen **dem** / **der** / **den** Kirche (*f*) und **dem** / **der** / **den** Käsegeschäft (*nt*).

....

4 Der Stoff hängt hinter **dem** / **der** / **den** Bett (*nt*).

....

5 In **diesem** / **dieser** / **diesen** Geschäft (*nt*) verkauft man schöne Schuhe.

....

6 Meine Tasche liegt unter **dem** / **der** / **den** Tisch (*m*).

....

G

Dual-case prepositions can be followed by the **accusative** if movement is implied or by the **dative** if no movement is implied.

an on (the wall)
auf on (the bed)
hinter behind
in in
neben next to
über over
unter under
vor in front of
zwischen between

Use the glossary to look up any words that are unfamiliar, and try to learn them.

H 6 Translate these sentences into German.

1 I find the app very easy but not always cheap.

....

2 I don't like shopping online because you can't try the things.

....

3 Yesterday afternoon I bought a lovely new bag.

....

4 You can find everything in the supermarkets.

....

In a different context, you may have learned this German word as meaning 'narrow'.

5 I have to buy new shoes because my shoes are too tight.

....

4 Mein idealer Wohnort

• F Using a range of tenses • F Using *ich möchte*

1 Draw lines to match up the German with the English nouns.

1 der Baum	a town
2 die Küste	b house
3 die Wohnung	c tree
4 das Haus	d village
5 das Dorf	e coast
6 die Stadt	f neighbour
7 die Pflanze	g flat
8 der Nachbar	h plant

2 Complete these sentences with the correct imperfect tense form of the verb in brackets.

1 Ich .... eine kleine Wohnung dort. (*haben*)
2 Ich .... sehr glücklich. (*sein*)
3 Er .... in einem großen Haus wohnen. (*wollen*)
4 Es .... viele Bäume. (*geben*)
5 Wir .... eine moderne Wohnung. (*haben*)
6 Ich .... das Haus kaufen. (*wollen*)

G
The **perfect tense** is used in spoken German and in more informal writing.
*Ich **habe** in der Schweiz **gewohnt**.*
I **lived** in Switzerland.
The **imperfect tense** is used in written narrative accounts, stories and reviews.
*ich **war*** I was
*ich **hatte*** I had
*es **gab*** there was, there were
Look back at page 62 of this workbook for a reminder of modal verbs in the imperfect tense.

3 Underline the verbs in each sentence. Then translate the verbal phrases into English.

1 Ich möchte im Ausland leben. ....
2 Ich möchte eine Aktivität mit anderen jungen Personen machen.
....
3 Ich möchte in einem Dorf wohnen. ....
4 Der Erwachsene möchte an der Küste leben. ....
5 Er möchte an einen privaten Strand gehen. ....
6 Meine Pflanze ist tot und ich möchte eine neue Pflanze kaufen. ....
....

G
To say what you **would like to** do, use *möchte* with a second verb (infinitive) at the end of the clause.
*Ich **möchte** in einer Wohnung **wohnen**.*
I **would like to live** in an apartment.

4 Translate these sentences into English on a separate sheet.

1 Ich wohne in einer modernen Wohnung.
2 Ich lebe gern hier, weil es sehr grün ist.
3 Ich finde das Dorf sehr langweilig.
4 Als ich jünger war, habe ich in einer Stadt gewohnt.
5 Ich möchte in Deutschland leben.

4 Mein idealer Wohnort (1)

H Using regular verbs in the imperfect tense

H 1 Complete these sentences by translating the word in brackets into German.

1 Es gibt viele .... (*activities*) für junge Leute.

2 Es gibt einige .... (*trees*).

3 Es gibt .... (*plants*) im Garten.

4 In der Schweiz gibt es viele schöne .... (*towns*).

5 Die .... (*apartments*) sind sehr groß.

6 Die .... (*houses*) sind sehr modern.

G

H The **imperfect tense** is used mainly in written narrative accounts and stories to describe an event in the past.
For regular verbs in the imperfect tense, form the stem by removing *-en* from the end of the infinitive, then add the imperfect tense endings.
When a verb stem ends in *-t*, just remove *-n*:
*war**ten*** ⟶ *war**te**-* ⟶ *ich war**tete***
Depending on the context, the imperfect tense can be translated in different ways:
Ich lernte Deutsch. I learned German. / I used to learn German. / I was learning German.

ich	mach**te**
du	mach**test**
er/sie/es/man	mach**te**
wir	mach**ten**
ihr	mach**tet**
Sie	mach**ten**
sie	mach**ten**

H 2 Rewrite these sentences, putting the verb into the imperfect tense.

1 In meinem Zimmer tanze ich. ....

2 Ich spiele Handball. ....

3 Ich mache die Aufgabe. ....

4 Sie kauft oft Bücher. ....

5 Er hört nicht gern Musik. ....

6 Wir arbeiten im Haus. ....

H 3 Complete these German translations by putting the verbs in brackets into the correct form of the imperfect tense.

1 I asked my mum. *Ich* .... (*fragen*) *meine Mutter.*

2 He often laughed. *Er* .... (*lachen*) *oft.*

3 She loved the book. *Sie* .... (*lieben*) *das Buch.*

4 We hated the school. *Wir* .... (*hassen*) *die Schule.*

5 I worked in an office. *Ich* .... (*arbeiten*) *in einem Büro.*

6 He said 'yes'. *Er* .... (*sagen*) *„Ja".*

7 Did you want to meet somebody? .... (*Wollen*) *du jemanden treffen?*

H 4 Translate these sentences into German on a separate sheet.

1 I used to dance at school.

2 I loved the film.

3 She often bought clothes.

4 We always asked the teacher.

5 They hated the series.

4 Mein idealer Wohnort (2)

H Using irregular verbs in the imperfect tense

H 1 These imperfect tense verbs are all in the *ich, er/sie/es/man* forms. Draw lines to match them up with their infinitive.

1 fiel	**a** sehen
2 starb	**b** helfen
3 sah	**c** fallen
4 kam	**d** gehen
5 half	**e** nehmen
6 ging	**f** sterben
7 blieb	**g** kommen
8 nahm	**h** bleiben

G

H Many verbs are irregular in the imperfect tense. Here are some examples:

	infinitive	**imperfect tense (*ich, er/sie/es/man* forms)**
to bring	bringen	brachte
to think	denken	dachte
to find	finden	fand
to go, drive	fahren	fuhr
to win	gewinnen	gewann
to read	lesen	las
to leave	lassen	ließ
to like	mögen	mochte

The *wir/Sie/sie* forms add -(*e*)*n*.

H 2 Circle all the imperfect tense verbs in this text. On a separate sheet, list them and translate them into English.

laut *according to*
zunehmen *to increase*

There are 17 different imperfect tense verbs in the text in exercise 2.
Look out for common irregular verbs that may be more familiar to you:
haben ⟶ *hatte*   *sein* ⟶ *war*   *gehen* ⟶ *ging*
If you spot others in the text that you don't know the meaning of, look them up in the glossary at the end of the module.

Eine Beschreibung von meinem Leben

Als ich jünger war, wohnte ich in einer Stadt im Norden. Die Bevölkerung da nahm immer zu, aber laut meiner Mutter blieb die Umgebung sehr ruhig. Ich ging zu Fuß in die Schule, fünfmal jede Woche. Ich nahm nie den Bus – ein Zeichen, dass ich in Form bleiben wollte. Ich blieb sechs Jahre in der Grundschule. Jedenfalls wusste ich, dass die Schule sehr gut war. Ich sprach ein bisschen Deutsch, weil unser Lehrer aus Deutschland kam. Schade, dass ich aber nur Englisch schrieb. Meine Mutter war diejenige, die mir mit den Hausaufgaben half. Zu Abend aß ich mit meiner Familie und danach saß ich im Wohnzimmer und sah fern. Um zehn Uhr schlief ich. Mit elf Jahren zog ich in ein neues Haus im Westen, und mit achtzehn Jahren ging ich von der Schule ab.

H 3 Translate these sentences into English on a separate sheet.

1 Er sprach Englisch.
2 Ich mochte die Serie.
3 Er gewann ein Buch.
4 Sie half ihrem Vater.
5 Er brachte ein Geschenk.
6 Er gab es seinem Vater.
7 Wir aßen fast ein Kilogramm Pommes.
8 Mochtest du deine Nachbarn?

H 4 Translate these sentences into German on a separate sheet, using the imperfect tense.

1 He took the plant.
2 I thought it was good.
3 She stayed at home.
4 I saw the house.
5 We wrote a text.
6 I knew that it was difficult.

4 Mein idealer Wohnort (3)

H Revising the conditional

H 1 Translate these sentences into English.

1 Ich möchte in diese Richtung fahren. ....

2 Möchtest du ins Geschäft gehen? ....

3 Er möchte Zeit sparen. ....

4 Sie möchte die Produkte verkaufen. ....

5 Wir möchten den Käse probieren. ....

6 Sie möchten Obst essen. ....

> **G**
> H You can use the **imperfect subjunctive** form of ***mögen*** to say 'would like'.
> *Ich **möchte** eine Jacke.* I would like a jacket.
> *Ich **möchte** eine Jacke **kaufen**.*
> I would like to buy a jacket.

H 2 Complete each German translation with the missing verb.

1 The garden would be very green.

Der Garten .... sehr grün.

2 The town would have lots of trees and plants.

Die Stadt .... viele Bäume und Pflanzen.

3 I would like to live in Austria.

Ich .... gern in Österreich leben.

4 My dad would be very angry.

Mein Vater .... sehr böse.

5 I would like a horse.

Ich .... ein Pferd.

6 We would like to move to a bigger house.

Wir .... gern in ein größeres Haus ziehen.

> **G**
> H To form the **conditional**, use **würde** with an **infinitive**:
> *Ich **würde tanzen**.* I would dance.
> *Er **würde** das Haus **verlassen**.*
> He would leave the house.
> You can use *würde* with *gern* to mean 'would like':
> *Ich **würde gern** in Deutschland leben.*
> I would like to live in Germany.
> In Module 4, you met ***wäre*** and ***hätte*** in sentences like these:
> *Wenn ich müde wäre, würde ich schlafen.*
> If I were tired, I would sleep.
> *Wenn ich Hunger hätte, würde ich essen.*
> If I were hungry, I would eat.
> ***wäre*** can also mean 'would be':
> *Es **wäre** modern.* It would be modern.
> ***hätte*** can also mean 'would have':
> *Mein Haus **hätte** drei Schlafzimmer.*
> My house would have three bedrooms.
> Note also: ***Es gäbe*** *einen Garten.*
> **There would be** a garden.

H 3 Translate these sentences into English on a separate sheet.

1 Ich würde gern in die Stadt gehen.

2 Die Produkte würden direkt nach Hause kommen.

3 Das Dorf wäre sehr schön.

4 Es gäbe viele Leute.

5 Sie würde in einem neuen Geschäft einkaufen.

6 Er würde eine Fahrkarte kaufen.

H 4 Translate these sentences into German on a separate sheet.

1 I like living in a modern house.

2 When I was younger, I lived in a village.

3 According to my dad it was very pretty but there weren't many activities.

4 In the future I would like to live in a village.

5 It would be quite big and it would have a shop, a pretty park and a café.

5 Bei mir zu Hause

- Using prepositions with the accusative and the dative
- Working out the meaning of compound nouns

1 Use your knowledge of compound nouns to work out the English meanings of these home-related words.

G German often combines two or more words to make new nouns. These are called **compound nouns**. They combine two nouns, a verb stem and a noun, or an adjective and a noun.

1 das Arbeitszimmer ....

2 das Musikzimmer ....

3 das Wohnzimmer ....

4 das Badezimmer ....

5 das Spielzimmer ....

6 der Weinkeller ....

7 die Essecke ....

H **8** die Waschmaschine ....

2 Draw lines to match up the sentences with the rooms.

1 Hier ziehe ich mich an.	**a** das Badezimmer
2 Hier arbeite ich.	**b** das Büro
3 Hier spiele ich Fußball.	**c** das Wohnzimmer
4 Hier nehme ich ein Bad.	**d** das Schlafzimmer
5 Hier sehe ich fern.	**e** der Garten
6 Hier gibt es einen Vogel.	**H** **f** das Dach

G Some **prepositions** are followed by the **accusative** when there is movement towards an object and the **dative** if there is no movement towards an object.

an on (the wall)	*über* over
auf on (the bed)	*unter* under
hinter behind	*vor* in front of
in in	*zwischen* between
neben next to	

H *Wir hängen das Bild* ***an die*** *Wand.* We're hanging the picture on the wall.

Das Bild hängt ***an der*** *Wand.* The picture is hanging on the wall.

★ Some prepositions and definite articles are shortened into one word:

an + das → *ans*
auf + das → *aufs*
in + das → *ins*
in + dem → *im*

3 Underline the preposition in each sentence. Decide if there is movement towards an object or no movement towards an object and write down the case used after the preposition.

1 Ich stelle den Tisch auf den Boden. ....

2 Die Stühle stehen vor dem Tisch. ....

3 Die Wohnung liegt im Dorf. ....

4 Die Toilette ist im Badezimmer. ....

H **5** Ich hänge die Jacke an die Tür. ....

H **6** Die Bilder hängen an der Wand. ....

H **7** Ich habe auf dem Bett gesessen. ....

Notice the difference between this sentence and: *Ich habe mich aufs Bett gesetzt.* The cases will help you work out which means 'was seated/sitting' and which means 'sat down'.

4 Complete these sentences with the correct form of the definite article.

1 Ich schlafe in .... Schlafzimmer.

2 Der Stuhl liegt neben .... Tisch.

3 Ich gehe in .... Schlafzimmer.

4 Der Gast kommt zu .... Feier.

5 Ich stelle die Waschmaschine hinter .... Tür.

H 6 Heute ziehen wir in .... neue Haus.

> **G** The verb is always the second idea of a German sentence. This means if something else comes first, then the **verb** and the subject must swap over.
> *Unten/Links* ***gibt*** *es vier Zimmer.* Downstairs / On the left there are four rooms.
> *Hinten/Rechts* ***gibt*** *es einen Garten.* Behind / On the right there is a garden.
> *Oben* ***gibt*** *es drei Schlafzimmer.* Upstairs there are three bedrooms.

H 5 Rewrite each sentence, putting the words into the correct order. Start with the 'place' element.

1 es gibt Unten zwei Zimmer ....

2 es Hinten gibt Mauer eine ....

3 Oben Schlafzimmer es gibt vier ....

4 fern sehe Wohnzimmer Im ich ....

5 Hier Waschmaschine eine es gibt ....

6 Garten spiele Tennis ich mit Bruder meinem Im ....

....

F 6 Translate these sentences into German.

1 I work in the office. ....

2 I like living here because the house is lovely. ....

....

3 I get dressed in the bedroom in the morning. ....

....

4 Upstairs we have four bedrooms. ....

5 Yesterday I worked in the kitchen. ....

H 7 Translate these sentences into English.

1 Gestern bin ich in ein neues Haus gezogen. ....

2 Unten haben wir vier Zimmer und oben haben wir fünf Schlafzimmer. ....

....

3 Wir haben den Tisch in die Küche gestellt. ....

4 Es gibt auch vier Stühle vor dem Tisch. ....

5 An die Wände haben wir unsere alten Bilder und viele Fotos gehangen. ....

....

Glossary

bold = this word will appear in Higher exams only

ab (adv)	*off, away*
ab (prep)	*from, as of*
Ahnung (f)	*idea, suspicion*
als	*than, (also: when, as)*
am	*on the, at the (m, nt) (dative) /* ***in the process of, during / while***
an	*on, at*
angenehm	*pleasant*
ans	*on(to) the, at the (nt) (accusative)*
anziehen; sich acc. anziehen; sich dat. + noun anziehen	*(to) attract, put on | attracting, putting on; (to) get dressed | getting dressed; (to) put on + noun | putting on + noun*
aß	*(I, she, he, it) ate*
auf	*on, onto, at, to*
aus	*out, out of, from*
außer	*except, apart from*
Auto (nt)	*car*
Bahn (f)	*train, railway*
Bahnhof (m)	*(railway) station*
Bank (f)	*bank, bench*
Bau (m)	*construction, building*
bei	*at (the house of), with /* ***in the process of, during/while***
beim	*at (the house of) the, with the (m, nt) /* ***in the process of, during/while***
Bereich (m)	*area, region, district*
Bericht (m)	*report, record*
Beschreibung (f)	*description*
Bevölkerung (f)	*population, people, members of the public*
bis	*until, till, up to, by*
blieb	*(I, she, he, it) remained, stayed*
Boden (m)	*ground, floor, bottom*
brachte	*(I, she, he, it) brought*
breit	*wide, broad*
Brücke (f)	*bridge*
Büro (nt)	*office*
Bus (m)	*bus*
Busse (pl)	*buses*
Dach (nt)	*roof*
dachte	*(I, she, he, it) thought*
derjenige, diejenige, dasjenige	*the one (who, that)*
direkt	*direct, straight, directly, immediately*
Dorf (m)	*village*
dort	*there*
durch	*through*
Ecke (f)	*corner*
einige	*a few, some*
Einwohner (m)	*inhabitant, resident*
einzig	*only, single*
eng	*narrow, close, tight*
entfernt	*distant, away*
entlang	*along*
entschuldigen; sich acc. entschuldigen (bei ...)	*(to) excuse | excusing; (to) apologise (to someone) | apologising*
Entschuldigung (f)	*apology, excuse, excuse me, sorry*

erreichen	*(to) achieve, reach / achieving, reaching*			
Erwachsene (m) (f)	*adult, grown-up*			
Fahrrad (nt)	*bicycle*			
Fahrt (f)	*drive, trip*			
Fahrzeug (nt)	*vehicle*			
Feld (nt)	*field, pitch, court (sport)*			
fern	*far, distant*			
fiel	*(I, she, he, it) fell, decreased*			
fliegen	*(to) fly / flying*			
Flughafen (m)	*airport*			
Flugzeug (nt)	*aeroplane, plane, aircraft*			
frisch	*fresh, freshly*			
fuhr	*(I, she, he, it) travelled, drove*			
führen	*(to) lead, guide / leading, guiding*			
für	*for*			
gab	*(I, she, he, it) gave*			
Garten (m)	*garden*			
Gast (m)	*guest (m), visitor*			
Gebiet (nt)	*region, area, territory*			
gegen	*against*			
Gegend (f)	*area, region*			
gegenüber	*opposite, across from*			
Geschäft (nt)	*business, shop*			
(aux) ... geschlossen	*closed, shut*			
(aux) ... gesessen	*sat / (have, has) sat (pp)*			
Geschwindigkeit (f)	*speed*			
gewann	*(I, she, he, it) won*			
(aux) ... gezogen	*pulled, moved / (have, has) pulled, moved (pp)*			
ging	*(I, she, he, it) went*			
Größe (f)	*size, height*			
half	*(I, she, he, it) helped*			
hängen	*(to) hang / hanging*			
hässlich	*ugly, hideous*			
Hauptstadt (f)	*capital city*			
Haus (nt)	*house*			
her	*from something, ago, as far as ... is concerned*			
hinten	*at/in the back*			
hinter	*behind*			
hoch	*high, tall*			
Höhe (f)	*height, altitude*			
im	*in the (m, nt) (dative)*			
in	*in, into*			
ins	*into the (nt) (accusative)*			
je	*ever, each*			
jedenfalls	*in any case, at any rate, anyhow*			
jemand	*someone (subj)*			
jemanden	*someone (obj)*			
Jugendliche (pl), (die) Jugendlichen	*young people, (the) young people*			
jung	*young*			
kam	*(I, she, he, it) came*			
Keller (m)	*cellar, basement*			
Kilo(gramm), kg (nt)	*kilo(gram)*			
Kirche (f)	*church*			
Kleidung (f)	*clothes, outfit*			
kommen	*(to) come / coming*			
König (m)	*king*			
Kosten (pl)	*costs, expenses*			
kosten	*(to) cost / costing*			
kulturell	*cultural*			
Laden (m)	*shop*			

Lage (f)	*situation, location, position*
Land (nt)	*land, country, state, countryside*
Landschaft (f)	*landscape, countryside*
las	*(I, she, he, it) read*
laut	*according to*
leben	*(to) live | living*
Leben (nt)	*life*
ließ	*(I, she, he, it) let, allowed*
linke (r, s)	*left*
links	*on/to the left*
Maschine (f)	*machine*
Mauer (f)	*wall*
meist	*most, mostly, usually*
meiste	*most*
Meter, m (m)	*metre*
mit	*with, by*
mitnehmen	*(to) take along | taking along*
Mitte (f)	*middle, centre*
mochte	*(I, she, he, it, one) liked*
mochtest	*(you (sing informal)) liked*
Moschee (f)	*mosque*
Museum (nt)	*museum*
nach	*to, towards, after, according to*
Nachbar (m)	*neighbour*
Nähe (f)	*vicinity, proximity*
nahe, nah	*near(by), close*
nahm	*(I, she, he, it) took, had something to eat or drink*
national	*national*
neben	*next to, beside*
niedrig	*low*

Norden (m), Nord-	*north*
offen	*open*
öffentlich	*public*
Öffentlichkeit (f)	*public*
ohne	*without*
Ort (m)	*place, town, location*
Osten (m), Ost-	*east*
passen	*(to) fit, suit | fitting, suiting*
Pflanze (f)	*plant*
Post (f) (m)	*post, mail, post office (f), (blog) post (m)*
Preis (m)	*price, prize, award*
privat	*private, personal*
pro	*per*
Rand (m)	*edge*
rechte (r, s)	*right*
rechts	*on/to the right*
Richtung (f)	*direction, way*
sah	*(I, she, he, it) saw*
saß	*(I, she, he, it) sat*
schade	*(it's a) pity, (it's a) shame*
Schiff (nt)	*ship*
schlief	*(I, she, he, it) slept*
schrieb	*(I, she, he, it) wrote*
sprach	*(I, she, he, it) spoke, talked*
Sprache (f)	*language, speech*
Stadion (nt)	*stadium*
Stadt (f)	*town, city*
starb	*(I, she, he, it) died*
stellen; sich acc. stellen	*(to) place, set, put | placing, setting, putting; (to) place oneself, stand | placing oneself, standing*

Stoff (m)	*material, substance, fabric*
Straßenbahn (f)	*tram*
Süden (m), Süd-	*south*
Supermarkt (m)	*supermarket*
Synagoge (f)	*synagogue*
Tasche (f)	*pocket, bag*
Tempel (m)	*temple*
Toilette (f)	*toilet*
tot	*dead*
U-Bahn (f)	*underground railway, metro*
über	*about, above, over*
um	*at (o'clock), around*
Umgebung (f)	*surroundings, neighbourhood*
unten	*down, downstairs, below*
unter	*under, below, among*
Verbindung (f)	*connection, link*
verkaufen	*(to) sell | selling*
Verkehr (m)	*traffic, transport*
vom	*from the, of the (m, nt)*
von	*from, of*
vor	*in front of, before, ago*
Wand (f)	*wall*
weißt	*(you (sing informal)) know (something)*
Westen (m), West-	*west*
wissen	*(to) know (something) | knowing (something) / (we/they/you (formal)) know (something)*
wohnen	*(to) live, stay (holidays) | living, staying (holidays)*
Wohnung (f)	*apartment, flat*
Wohnzimmer (nt)	*living room, lounge, sitting room*
wolltest	*(you (sing informal)) wanted (to)*
wusste	*(I, she, he, it) knew*
Zeichen (nt)	*sign, symbol*
Zentimeter, cm (m)	*centimetre, cm*
ziehen	*(to) pull, move | pulling, moving*
zog	*(I, she, he, it) pulled, moved*
zu (adv)	*too*
zu (prep)	*to*
Zug (m)	*train*
zum, zur	*to the (m, nt), to the (f)*
zunehmen	*(to) increase, put on weight | increasing, putting on weight*
zurück	*back*
zwischen	*between*

Foundation translation revision

German to English

1 Circle the odd one out.

1 Hose / T-Shirt / Schuhe / Hemd

2 Montag / Mathe / Kunst / Englisch

3 Laptop / Bilder / Handy / Telefon

4 Tante / Onkel / Oma / Stiefmutter

5 Brot / Wasser / Obst / Gemüse

2 Draw lines to match up the German sentences with their English translations.

1 In der Schule mache ich Sport.

2 In meiner Freizeit höre ich manchmal Musik.

3 Ich verstehe mich gar nicht gut mit meinem Bruder, der sehr laut ist.

4 Ich schlafe nicht genug, weil ich zu spät ins Bett gehe.

5 Letztes Wochenende habe ich im Kleidungsgeschäft eine neue Hose gekauft.

a In my free time I sometimes listen to music.

b I don't sleep enough because I go to bed too late.

c At school I do sport.

d Last weekend I bought a new pair of trousers in the clothes shop.

e I don't get on at all well with my brother, who is very loud.

3 Complete these sentences by translating the words in brackets into English.

1 .... (*Am Montag*) in the first lesson I have .... (*Musik*).

2 In .... (*meiner Freizeit*) I often stream .... (*Videos*).

3 I .... (*verstehe mich ziemlich gut*) with my mum who is very .... (*ruhig*).

4 I .... (*verbringe*) too much time on my .... (*Handy*).

5 .... (*Am Wochenende*) I bought .... (*ein Geschenk*) in the town centre.

4 Translate these sentences into English.

1 In der Schule lerne ich Mathe. ....

2 In meiner Freizeit sehe ich oft Filme. ....

3 Ich verstehe mich gut mit meiner Freundin, die sehr nett ist.

....

4 Ich esse ungesund, weil ich Pommes mag.

....

5 Gestern habe ich im Schuhgeschäft neue Schuhe gekauft.

....

English to German

1 Draw lines to match up the English with the German words.

1 school uniform	**a** die Sendungen
2 swimming	**b** das Spazierengehen
3 programmes	**c** das Schwimmen
4 stepfather	**d** der Stiefvater
5 walking	**e** die Schuluniform

2 Complete each German translation using a word from the box.

Komödien Woche laufen Zimmer spazieren

1 I go walking very often.	*Ich gehe sehr oft ....*
2 I think the room is too quiet.	*Ich finde das .... zu ruhig.*
3 I like comedies because they're really funny.	*Ich mag ...., denn sie sind wirklich lustig.*
4 At the weekend I will go running in the park.	*Ich werde am Wochenende im Park .... gehen.*
5 Last week I went to a big party.	*Letzte .... bin ich auf eine große Party gegangen.*

3 Circle the correct option to complete each German translation.

1 I swim three times a week.	*Ich schwimme* ***manchmal / dreimal*** *pro Woche.*
2 I find this rule quite right.	*Ich finde diese Regel ganz* ***wichtig / richtig****.*
3 I dislike sports programmes because they're quite boring.	*Ich mag Sportsendungen nicht, weil sie ganz* ***langweilig / toll*** *sind.*
4 I will play football in the park with my friend later.	*Ich werde später mit meiner Freundin im Park* ***Basketball / Fußball*** *spielen.*
5 Last month we celebrated my mum's birthday.	***Letzte Woche / Letzten Monat*** *haben wir den Geburtstag von meiner Mutter gefeiert.*

4 Translate these sentences into German.

1 I play tennis twice a week.

....

2 I think that the school rules are right.

....

3 I like soap operas because they're particularly exciting.

....

4 At the weekend I will go shopping with my friend in the town centre.

....

5 Last year we celebrated my birthday at home.

....

Higher translation revision

German to English

1 Circle the odd one out.

1 Direktor / Lehrer / Schauspieler / Schüler

2 gerecht / schön / praktisch / unbequem

3 Krimi / Ausstellung / Serie / Seifenoper

4 Laptop / Handy / Telefon / Vorstellung

5 Eigenschaft / Kontakt / Verständnis / Beziehung

2 Draw lines to match up the German sentences with their English translations.

1 Ich finde diese Regel nicht gerecht.

2 Ich sehe ab und zu Serien, denn die Geschichten sind interessant.

3 Ich bin nicht gesund, weil ich mich nicht genug bewege.

4 Ich habe schlechte Beziehungen zu meinen Eltern.

5 Letztes Wochenende haben wir im Garten zusammen gegessen.

a I have bad relationships with my parents.

b I watch series now and again because the stories are interesting.

c Last weekend we ate together in the garden.

d I find this rule unfair.

e I'm not healthy because I don't exercise enough.

3 Correct the English translations by crossing through the incorrect words and writing the corrections above or next to them.

1 Mir gefällt meine Schule.

I dislike my school.

2 Ich bin der Meinung, dass die Schulregeln ungerecht sind.

I'm of the opinion that the school rules are fair.

3 Zu Hause streame ich oft Filme, denn es gibt viel Spannung in den Filmen.

At home I often stream videos because there is a lot of tension in the videos.

4 Ich verbringe viel Zeit mit meinen Freundinnen, obwohl ich mich auch gut mit meinen Schwestern verstehe.

I spend little time with my friend, although I also get on well with my sisters.

5 Letzten Sommer sind wir zusammen zum Strand gegangen.

Last autumn we went to the lake together.

4 Translate these sentences into English on a separate sheet.

1 Mir gefällt die Schule nicht, weil die Stunden langweilig sind.

2 Ich finde den Direktor extrem gerecht und immer freundlich.

3 Zu Hause sehen wir häufig Serien an, denn die Schauspieler sind sehr gut.

4 Ich habe gute Beziehungen zu meinen Eltern, obwohl sie streng sind.

5 Am Wochenende sind wir im Park spazieren gegangen.

English to German

1 Draw lines to match up the English with the German words.

1 atmosphere	**a** die Vorstellung
2 offer	**b** die Ausstellung
3 exhibition	**c** der Verein
4 club	**d** die Stimmung
5 performance	**e** das Angebot

2 Complete each German translation using a word from the box.

gab spielen
hochgeladen
konnte angeschaut

1 *Yesterday I uploaded photos to social media.*	Gestern habe ich Fotos in sozialen Medien ....
2 *Last weekend I watched a series which was very funny.*	Letztes Wochenende habe ich eine Serie ...., die sehr lustig war.
3 *In the film there was a lot of tension.*	Im Film .... es viel Spannung.
4 *I couldn't work because I was very tired.*	Ich .... nicht arbeiten, weil ich sehr müde war.
5 *Tomorrow I will go to the tennis club and play with my friends.*	Morgen werde ich zum Tennisverein gehen und mit meinen Freunden ....

3 Circle the correct option to complete each German translation.

1 *Yesterday I had lots of work.*	**Gestern hatte ich / Heute habe ich** viel Arbeit.
2 *The work was very difficult.*	Die Arbeit war sehr **leicht / schwierig**.
3 *I couldn't work.*	Ich **kannte / konnte** nicht arbeiten.
4 *I downloaded some photos.*	Ich habe einige **Freunde eingeladen / Fotos heruntergeladen**.
5 *We are preparing an exhibition.*	Wir bereiten eine **Vorstellung / Ausstellung** vor.

4 Translate these sentences into German.

1 Yesterday I had lots of homework and the exercises were very difficult.

....

2 I couldn't concentrate very well.

....

3 Afterwards I downloaded a film which I watched on the computer.

....

4 The film had a good atmosphere but there was violence.

....

5 Tonight I will go to the theatre club where we are preparing a performance.

....

Kulturzone Im Urlaub und unterwegs

F Using adjectival endings after the definite article

1 Tick the correct English translation: a or b.

1 bauen
- **a** to like ☐
- **b** to build ☐

2 beantworten
- **a** to ask ☐
- **b** to answer ☐

3 besuchen
- **a** to visit ☐
- **b** to see ☐

4 kommen
- **a** to come ☐
- **b** to go ☐

5 empfehlen
- **a** to look for ☐
- **b** to recommend ☐

6 zeigen
- **a** to draw ☐
- **b** to show ☐

G

Adjective endings change after the definite article according to the case.

	nominative endings	**accusative endings**
masculine	**Der** lang**e** Fluss ist der Rhein.	Ich sehe **den** lang**en** Fluss.
feminine	**Die** ganz**e** Welt kommt nach Deutschland.	Ich reise um **die** ganz**e** Welt.
neuter	**Das** interessant**e** Schloss ist in der Nähe von Berlin.	Es gibt **das** interessant**e** Schloss.
plural	**Die** traditionell**en** Besucher kommen aus der Schweiz.	Es gibt **die** traditionell**en** Besucher.

The endings don't change the meaning of the word! *Lang*, *lange* and *langen* all translate as 'long'.

2 Circle the adjective in each sentence. Write which case it is in and translate it into English.

1. Das ist ein sehr beliebtes Schloss. ....
2. Ich sehe den hohen Berg. ....
3. Der lange Fluss geht durch die Stadt. ....
4. Es gibt das historische Tor. ....
5. Die traditionellen Touristen kommen im August. ....
6. Der bequeme Stuhl ist braun. ....

The adjective *hoh-* is a form of *hoch*. Can you remember what this adjective means?

3 Complete these sentences with the correct form of the adjective in brackets.

1. Der .... Wald liegt in der Stadt. (*alt*)
2. Ich sehe das .... Schloss oben auf dem Berg. (*schön*)
3. Ich nehme den .... Weg geht durch den Park. (*kurz*)
4. Die .... Straße ist sehr bekannt. (*weit*)
5. Er hatte eine .... Reise. (*spannend*)

4 Translate these sentences into German on a separate sheet.

1. I like the castle.
2. You can see the town.
3. My best friend is from Switzerland.
4. I like the mountains because they're beautiful.
5. Last year I visited the historical town.

H 1 Complete each German sentence using a word from the box.

Gebäude Welt Region Informationen willkommen kommt

1 Meine beste Freundin .... aus Deutschland. *My best friend is from Germany.*

2 Ich muss die .... suchen. *I have to look for the information.*

3 Ich will um die .... reisen. *I want to travel around the world.*

4 Sie sind alle herzlich .... *You are all warmly welcome.*

5 Das ist ein sehr altes und riesiges .... *That's a very old and huge building.*

6 Ich wohne in einer sehr schönen .... *I live in a very beautiful region.*

G

H For instructions and recommendations, use the **imperative** form.
In a **formal** situation, use the *Sie* form of the verb followed by the word *Sie*.
Besuchen Sie *Deutschland im Sommer!*
Visit Germany in the summer!
Beantworten Sie *die Frage!*
Answer the question!

In **informal** situations, use *du* and *ihr*.
For one person, use the *du* form of the verb without the -*st* verb ending and omit *du*:
Mach *die Hausaufgaben!* Do your homework!
For more than one, use the *ihr* form and omit *ihr*:
Macht *die Hausaufgaben!* Do your homework!
sein has an irregular imperative form.
Sie: ***Seien*** *Sie klar!* Be clear! *du*: ***Sei*** *laut!* Be loud!
ihr: ***Seid*** *ruhig!* Be quiet!

Try to work out the meaning of the sentences in the exercises. Use the glossary at the end of the module to help.

H 2 Draw lines to match up each statement with the most likely imperative sentence.

1 Wir spielen unsere Musik wirklich laut.
2 Ich mag Geschichte am besten.
3 Ich habe ein Interview in meiner ehemaligen Schule.
4 Man braucht in dieser Region Fahrradwege.
5 Wir möchten in den Urlaub fahren.

a Fahrt in die Schweiz!
b Beschreib dann das letzte Jahrhundert!
c Seid ruhig!
d Mach einen großen Eindruck!
e Frag den Bürgermeister danach!

H 3 Complete these German sentences with the correct imperative form of the verb in brackets.

1 .... ruhig! (*Be – du*)
2 .... ein Schloss! (*Build – ihr*)
3 .... eine spannende Aktivität! (*Do – Sie*)
4 .... den höchsten Berg! (*Name – du*)
5 .... nicht Ihre liebsten Erinnerungen! (*Forget – Sie*)
6 .... im klaren blauen Wasser! (*Swim – ihr*)

nennen *to name*

H 4 Translate these sentences into English on a separate sheet.

1 Ich besuche diese Region gern, weil sie die wunderbarste ist.
2 In meinem Bereich gibt es viele hohe Berge und man kann wandern gehen.
3 Zu diesem Zeitpunkt gab es viele Schlösser in Deutschland.
4 Der ehemalige Bürgermeister war extrem beliebt, denn er war sehr freundlich.
5 Letztes Jahr habe ich eine Reise um die Welt gemacht.

1 Wo fahren wir hin?

- Forming questions
- Discussing advantages and disadvantages

1 Draw lines to match up the German with the English adjectives.

1 billig	**a** clean
2 echt	**b** exact
3 genau	**c** delicious
4 günstig	**d** favourable
5 lecker	**e** quiet
6 ruhig	**f** real
7 sauber	**g** cheap

2 Complete these sentences by translating the words in brackets into German.

1 Ich gehe bestimmt gern ins .... (*café*).

2 Ich mache extrem gern .... (*holidays*) in der frischen Luft.

3 Einer will zum .... (*beach*) gehen.

4 Das Restaurant liegt auf der linken .... (*side*).

5 Ich schwimme nicht gern im .... (*lake*).

6 Nehmen Sie die erste .... (*road*) rechts.

H 7 Insgesamt ist es unglaublich .... (*interesting*).

G

To form a yes/no question in German, swap over the **subject** and the verb.

Es *gibt Ruhe.*	→	*Gibt* ***es*** *Ruhe?*
There is peace.	→	Is there peace?
Das Wetter *ist gut.*	→	*Ist* ***das Wetter*** *gut?*
The weather is good.	→	Is the weather good?

3 Rewrite each question, putting the words into the correct order. Add a capital letter to the first word.

1 das du Essen magst? ....

2 die Wurst lecker ist? ....

3 nichts hast du Hause zu? ....

4 klar alles ist? ....

H 5 gilt Berg der als hoch? ....

H 6 dafür viel Kraft man braucht? ....

4 Complete these German sentences with the correct form of a modal verb and an infinitive from the box.

anbieten machen liegen schwimmen probieren

1 We are allowed to lie on the beach.	*Man* .... *am Strand* ....
2 We can do a tennis course.	*Man* .... *einen Tenniskurs* ....
3 We should swim in the lake.	*Man* .... *im See* ....

H **4** We must try the cake. *Man* .... *den Kuchen* ....

H **5** We can offer particular products. *Man* .... *bestimmte Produkte* ....

Use *man* (meaning 'we', 'you' or 'people) with **modal verbs** to talk about what everyone must, can, should, likes or is allowed to do. The *second* verb goes to the end of the clause in the infinitive form.
Man ***muss*** *antworten*. You must answer.
Man ***soll*** *ein Buch empfehlen*. You should recommend a book.
Man ***kann*** *im Restaurant essen*. We can eat in the restaurant.
Man ***darf*** *bestimmte Kleidung tragen*. We are allowed to wear certain clothes.

H 5 Read this German paragraph and complete the translation on the right.

Im Urlaub reise ich gern nach Deutschland. Man kann bestimmte Sachen sehen und die Museen sind echt interessant. Insbesondere muss man die hohen Berge und die tiefen Seen sehen. Sie sind völlig unglaublich und total schön!

In the holidays I **1** .... travelling to Germany. You **2** .... see certain **3** .... and the museums are **4** .... interesting. In particular you **5** .... see the **6** .... mountains and the **7** .... lakes. They are completely unbelievable and **8** .... lovely!

F 6 Translate these sentences into English.

1 Ich besuche Deutschland gern. ....

2 Das ist ein sehr sauberes Land. ....

3 Fährst du gern nach Österreich? ....

4 Man kann die hohen Berge sehen und sie sind wunderbar.

....

5 Letzten Sommer habe ich einen spannenden Besuch in die Schweiz gemacht.

....

H 7 Translate these sentences into German.

1 My excursion to Switzerland takes place next week.

....

2 I will visit five different cities.

....

3 I don't know exactly what high mountains there are.

....

4 When I am there, I will do a cookery course.

....

5 It's quite expensive but the buses are cheap.

....

2 Wo werden wir wohnen?

Using *wer*, *wen* and *wem* • Recognising negatives

1 Draw lines to match up the German with the English nouns.

1	das Bad	**a**	cuisine, kitchen
2	der Brief	**b**	husband, man
3	die Frau	**c**	letter
4	das Frühstück	**d**	centre
5	die Küche	**e**	bath, bathroom
6	der Mann	**f**	breakfast
7	das Zentrum	**g**	room
8	das Zimmer	**h**	wife, woman

2 Complete the German sentences using a word from the box.

praktisches Draußen Danke teuer Zimmer eigenes Linie für

1	Ich brauche ein	*I need a room.*
2	.... schön!	*Thank you very much!*
3	Das Zimmer ist nicht sehr	*The room is not very expensive.*
4	Was .... ein Hotel wollen Sie?	*What kind of hotel do you want?*
5	Das ist ein sehr .... Hotel.	*That is a very practical hotel.*
6	.... gibt es einen großen Garten.	*Outside there is a big garden.*
7	Sie hat ihr .... Zimmer.	*She has her own room.*
H 8	Sie hat nichts hinter der .... gemerkt.	*She didn't notice anything behind the line.*

3 Complete these sentences with the correct form of *wer*.

1 .... ist das?

2 Mit .... fahren Sie nach Deutschland?

3 Ohne .... reisen Sie?

4 Für .... ist das Zimmer?

5 Bei .... wohnen Sie?

6 .... spielt Tennis?

G

wer is an **interrogative** that changes its form depending on the case:

nominative	***Wer*** *braucht das Zimmer?* Who needs the room?
accusative	*Für* ***wen*** *wollen Sie das Zimmer?* For whom do you want the room?
dative	*Mit* ***wem*** *sind Sie?* Who are you with?

4 Underline the negative in each of these sentences. Then translate the sentences into English.

> **G** Learn to recognise negatives, as these change the meaning of the sentence.
> *ohne* without
> *kein* no, not a
> *nie* never
> *nicht* not
> *niemand* no-one
> *nichts* nothing
> **H** *weder … noch* neither … nor

1 Es gibt kein WLAN.

....

2 Die Zimmer sind nicht frei.

....

3 Niemand wohnt in einem Hotel.

....

H 4 Das Zimmer ist weder groß noch klein.

....

H 5 Sie hat nichts gemerkt.

....

H 6 Ich werde nie in einem Zelt schlafen.

....

H 5 Complete these sentences by translating the words in brackets into German.

1 Sie bittet nie um .... (*help*).

2 Wir brauchen kein .... (*tent*).

3 Am liebsten möchte ich in einem .... (*holiday house*) wohnen.

4 Ich bin nicht .... (*serious*).

5 Niemand .... (*remembers*) sich daran.

6 Mit .... (*whom*) werden Sie in der Ferienwohnung wohnen?

H 6 Translate these sentences into German.

1 I like staying in a hotel in the town centre. ....

2 Outside there is no garden. ....

3 No one wants wi-fi. ....

4 Who are you travelling with? ....

5 Last summer I stayed in a holiday apartment. ....

H 7 Translate these sentences into English.

1 Bitte schön, wer kommt mit? ....

2 Wir haben kein großes Zelt, aber wir haben ein Auto.

....

3 Ich möchte in einem Hotel bleiben, weil das bequemer ist.

....

4 Schwimmen ist meine Lieblingsaktivität, doch gibt es kein Wasser.

....

5 Letztes Wochenende haben wir in einer schlechten Ferienwohnung gewohnt.

....

Revising possessive adjectives

1 Match up the German words with the pictures. Write the correct letter.

1 der Blick ....

2 der Stuhl ....

3 das Telefon ....

4 das Bad ....

5 die Tür ....

6 das Fenster ....

7 das Ticket ....

8 das Bett ....

a

b
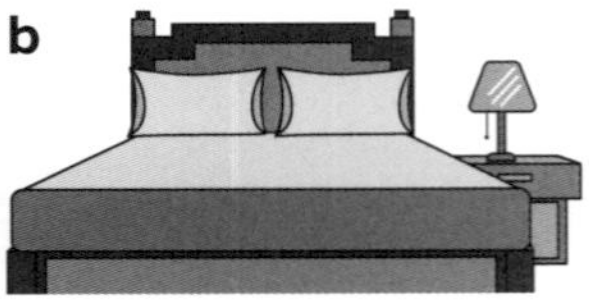

c

d

e

f

g
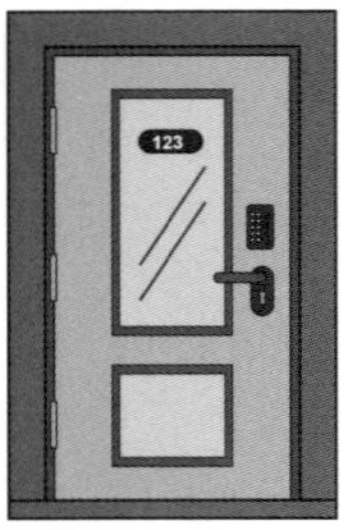

h

2 Circle the correct option to complete each English sentence.

1 Ich habe mein Ticket verloren. *I* ***lost*** */* ***found*** *my ticket.*

2 Das Geschäft hat geöffnet. *The shop* ***closed*** */* ***opened****.*

3 Das Fenster funktioniert nicht. *The window doesn't* ***work*** */* ***open****.*

4 Die Rechnung ist gar nicht klar. *The bill is not* ***right*** */* ***clear*** *at all.*

5 Das Bett ist kaputt. *The bed is* ***hard*** */* ***broken****.*

6 Die Mitarbeiter sind nicht höflich. *The employees are not* ***friendly*** */* ***polite****.*

7 Die Speisekarte ist schrecklich. *The menu is* ***terrible*** */* ***reasonable****.*

G

Remember that **possessive adjectives** change according to gender and case.
All possessive adjective endings follow the same pattern as the indefinite article.

	nominative	**accusative**
masc	mein	mein**en**
fem	meine	meine
neut	mein	mein
plural	meine	meine

subject pronoun	**possessive adjective**
ich	mein
du	dein
er/sie/es/man	sein-/ihr-/sein-
wir	unser
ihr	eu(e)r
Sie	Ihr
sie	ihr

3 Circle the correct possessive adjective to complete the sentences.

1 Nur **deinen** / **deine** / **dein** Bett (*nt*) ist schmutzig.

2 **Euren** / **Eure** / **Euer** Bad (*nt*) ist kaputt.

3 **Unseren** / **Unsere** / **Unser** Blick (*m*) ist nicht gut genug.

4 Zum Glück habe ich **meinen** / **meine** / **mein** Platz (*m*).

5 Plötzlich verliere ich **meinen** / **meine** / **mein** Geld (*nt*).

6 **Ihren** / **Ihre** / **Ihr** Zimmer ist nicht in Ordnung (*f*).

Use the glossary to look up any words that are unfamiliar, and try to learn them.

4 Complete each German sentence using a possessive adjective from the box.

Ihre deine ihrem unsere mein sein

gestohlen is the past participle of the verb *stehlen* (to steal).

1 Wir werden .... Rechnung (*f*) nicht bezahlen.	*We won't pay your bill.*
2 Leider ist .... Zimmer (*nt*) zu laut.	*Unfortunately, my room is too loud.*
3 Inzwischen haben Sie .... Tasche (*f*) verloren.	*In the meantime you lost your bag.*
H 4 Natürlich war sie nicht auf .... Flug (*m*).	*Of course she wasn't on her flight.*
H 5 Er war enttäuscht, weil .... Bett (*nt*) kaputt war.	*He was disappointed because his bed was broken.*
H 6 Glücklicherweise haben sie .... Schlüssel (*pl*) nicht gestohlen.	*Fortunately, they didn't steal our keys.*

H 5 Complete these sentences by translating the words in brackets into German.

1 Wir müssen für .... (*our damage*) bezahlen.
2 .... (*Their bus*) soll vor dem Hotel halten.
3 Sie kann .... (*her money*) nicht wechseln.
4 .... (*My*) Zimmer war in einem sehr schlechten .... (*condition*).
5 Sie verlangt ebenfalls .... (*our information*).
6 Er hat eben zu viel Lärm mit .... (*his music*) gemacht.

F 6 Translate these sentences into English.

1 Ich habe meine Kamera mit. ....
2 Mein Zimmer ist schmutzig. ....
3 Das Restaurant schließt um elf Uhr. ....
4 Die Mitarbeiter sind gar nicht freundlich. ....
5 Ich bin heute Abend angekommen. ....

H 7 Translate these sentences into German.

1 Fortunately my room is in order.

....

2 He came with nothing.

....

3 There's too much noise and I don't like it.

....

4 Someone has stolen my money.

....

5 His telephone is in a very bad condition.

....

4 Wie waren die Schulferien?

- Using past participles with inseparable prefixes
- **H** Using prepositions with the genitive

1 Draw lines to match up the English with the German nouns.

1 island	**a** das Grad
2 coast	**b** der Markt
3 sea	**c** die Reise
4 market	**d** die Insel
5 journey	**e** das Meer
6 sun	**f** die Küste
7 weather	**g** die Sonne
8 degree	**h** das Wetter

2 Match up the sentences with the weather symbols. Write the correct letter.

1 Hier war es kalt und es gab Wind. ....

2 Hier war es kalt und es hat geregnet. ....

3 Hier war es heiß und sonnig. ....

4 Hier war es kalt und sonnig. ....

5 Hier hat es geschneit. Es gab viel Schnee. ....

6 Hier hat es geregnet und es war warm. ....

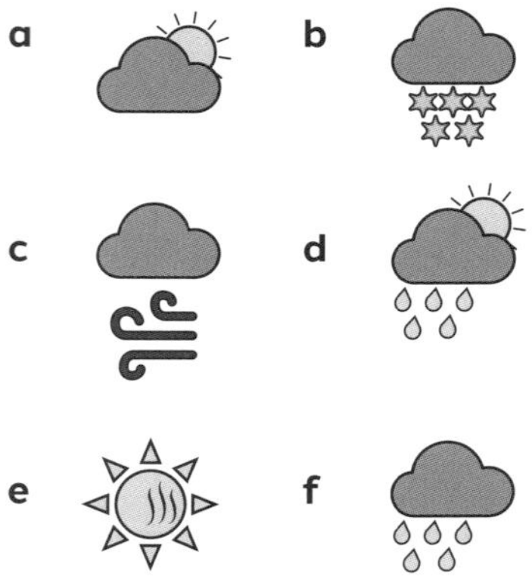

3 Underline the past participle in each sentence.

1 Ich bin auf dem Markt spazieren gegangen.

2 Unterwegs habe ich meine Tasche verloren.

3 Zuerst bin ich zu Hause geblieben.

4 Ich habe ein Eis bestellt.

5 Ich habe die Rechnung bezahlt.

6 Sie hat ihre Fotos vergessen.

G

Most verbs form their **past participle** by adding **ge-** and **-t** to the stem of the verb.

wohnen → *ich habe* ***ge****wohn****t***

Some verbs have inseparable prefixes (e.g. *be-* and *ver-*) and don't add *ge-* to the start of the verb. Some also don't change to *-t* at the end.

bestellen (to order) → *ich habe* ***be****stell****t***

bezahlen (to pay) → *ich habe* ***be****zahl****t***

verlieren (to lose) → *ich habe* ***ver****lor****en***

vergessen (to forget) → *ich habe* ***ver****gess****en***

4 Complete these sentences with the past participle of the verb in brackets.

1 Ich habe ein Museum .... (*besuchen*)

2 Sie haben Cola .... (*bestellen*)

3 Er hat sein Geld .... (*vergessen*)

4 Sie hat ihren Brief .... (*verlieren*)

5 Man hat die Kosten .... (*bezahlen*)

6 Seid ihr spazieren ....? (*gehen*)

G

H Some prepositions always take the **genitive** case in German.
während during, while, whereas
statt instead of
trotz despite
wegen because of

Note that for masculine and neuter nouns, you add *-s* to the end of the noun (or *-es* if the noun has one syllable): *während* ***des*** *Jahr**es*** during the year

	masc	fem	neut	pl
nominative	der	die	das	die
genitive	des	der	des	der

H 5 Complete these sentences with the correct form of the article. Then translate them into English.

1 Trotz .... Wetters lief ich.

....

2 Während .... Ferien habe ich niemanden gesehen.

....

3 Während .... Aufenthalts habe ich das Hotel gemocht.

....

4 Wegen .... Sonne war es aufregend.

....

5 Ich entschied, den Bus statt .... Straßenbahn zu nehmen.

....

6 Wegen .... Windes war das peinlich.

....

7 Bist du trotz .... Schnees zu Fuß hingegangen?

....

F 6 Translate these sentences into German.

1 I like staying in the mountains. ....

2 I often take photos because it's great.

....

3 I don't like to visit a museum because it's boring.

....

4 The weather was hot and sunny. ....

5 I stayed in a hotel. ....

H 7 Translate these sentences into English on a separate sheet.

1 Ich habe kein Geld übrig.

2 Das Wetter war heiß und es gab viel Sonne.

3 Die Anlage war groß und aufregend.

4 Ich bin zu Hause geblieben, obwohl das langweilig war.

5 Trotz des Wetters entschied ich, schwimmen zu gehen.

Use the glossary to look up any unfamiliar words and try to learn them.

5 Ich möchte um die Welt reisen!

Using interrogative and demonstrative adjectives

1 Unjumble the letters to write the German nouns correctly. Then translate the words into English.

1 rulKut ....
2 sKur ....
3 laM ....
4 kuftZun ....
5 einFer ....
6 blauUr ....
7 ssSloch ....
8 reeM ....

2 Complete each sentence using a verb from the box.

1 Wir werden viel Geld ....
2 Ich werde meine Familie ....
3 Sie wird die Ferien ....
4 Ihr werdet neue Leute ....
5 Ich will in der Sonne ....
6 Er will im Meer ....
7 Ich muss auf meine Schwester ....
8 Um wie viel Uhr möchtest du ....?

tauchen zurückkommen besuchen liegen genießen warten kennenlernen ausgeben

Use the glossary to look up any words that are unfamiliar and try to learn them.

3 Complete these German sentences with the correct form of the interrogative adjective (*welch-*).

1 .... Küche (*f*) ist besser? *Which cooking is better?*
2 .... Tag (*m*) ist es heute? *What day is it today?*
3 .... See (*f*) ist warm? *Which sea is warm?*
4 .... Meer (*nt*) ist kalt? *Which sea is cold?*
5 .... Berg (*m*) ist höher? *Which mountain is higher?*
6 .... Dörfer (*pl*) sind schön? *Which villages are lovely?*

The noun *See* has two meanings, depending on gender:
der *See* lake, ***die*** *See* sea

G

To say 'which ...?' in the nominative case, use the **interrogative adjective *welch-*** with the correct ending to agree with the noun that follows.

masc	***Welch<u>er</u>*** *Kurs ist besser?* Which course is better?	neut	***Welch<u>es</u>*** *Buch ist langweiliger?* Which book is more boring?
fem	***Welch<u>e</u>*** *Kultur ist interessanter?* Which culture is more interesting?	pl	***Welch<u>e</u>*** *Ferien sind idealer?* Which holidays are more ideal?

To say 'this ...' or 'these ...', use the **demonstrative adjective *dies-***, which follows the same pattern.

masc	***Dies<u>er</u>*** *Kurs ist besser.* This course is better.	neut	***Dies<u>es</u>*** *Buch ist langweiliger.* This book is more boring.
fem	***Dies<u>e</u>*** *Kultur ist interessanter.* This culture is more interesting.	pl	***Dies<u>e</u>*** *Ferien sind idealer.* These holidays are more ideal.

4 Complete these German sentences with the correct form of the demonstrative adjective (*dies-*).

1 .... Schlösser (*pl*) sind interessant. *These castles are interesting.*

2 .... See (*m*) ist kalt. *This lake is cold.*

3 .... Museum (*nt*) ist alt. *This museum is old.*

4 .... Kultur (*f*) ist fantastisch. *This culture is fantastic.*

5 .... Geschenk (*nt*) ist toll. *This present is great.*

H 6 .... Boot (*nt*) ist schnell. *This boat is fast.*

H 5 Complete these German sentences by translating the words in brackets.

1 Ich werde einen .... (*excursion*) zur Berliner Mauer machen.

2 Ich würde in der .... (*sun*) liegen.

3 Er will die .... (*culture*) entdecken.

4 Sie will in irgendein .... (*museum*) gehen.

5 Ich habe einen .... (*suggestion*) für dich.

6 Er würde ein .... (*problem*) vermeiden.

F 6 Translate these sentences into English.

1 Ich fahre wieder mit dem Schiff. ....

2 Wohin wirst du fahren? ....

3 Ich freue mich auf die Ferien. ....

4 Ich möchte im Meer schwimmen. ....

5 Letztes Jahr bin ich spazieren gegangen. ....

H 7 Translate these sentences into German.

1 I would like to do an excursion. ....

2 He wants to travel by boat. ....

Use the word *einige* for 'some'.

3 We will make some suggestions. ....

4 If I had time, I would discover the culture.

....

5 Last summer I went to Berlin and it was fun.

....

Glossary

bold = this word will appear in Higher exams only

alles klar	*that's fine, all right, okay, understood*
am besten	*(the) best (post-noun)*
anbieten	*(to) offer, serve something (with sth.) | offering, serving something (with sth.)*
ankommen (in dat. + noun)	*(to) arrive (at + noun) | arriving (at + noun)*
Anlage (f)	*facility, complex*
antworten (auf + noun)	*(to) answer (+ noun), respond, reply | answering (+ noun), responding, replying*
Aufenthalt (m)	*stay, residence*
aufregend	*exciting, thrilling*
Ausflug (m)	*excursion, trip, outing*
ausgeben	*(to) spend (money) | spending (money)*
Bad (nt)	*bath, bathroom, spa*
bauen	*(to) build, construct | building, constructing*
beantworten	*(to) answer | answering*
beliebt	*popular*
bequem	*comfortable*
Berg (m)	*mountain, hill*
Berliner (adj.)	*(of) Berlin*
beste	*best*
bestimmt	*certain, definite, certainly, definitely*
Besuch (m)	*visit*
besuchen	*(to) visit | visiting*
Besucher (m)	*visitor, guest*
Bett (nt)	*bed*
bezahlen	*(to) pay | paying*
bieten	*(to) offer, provide | offering, providing*
billig	*cheap, cheaply*
bitte	*please, you're welcome*
bitten um + noun	*(to) request + noun, ask for + noun | requesting + noun, asking for + noun*
Blick (m)	*look, view, glance*
Boot (nt)	*boat*
brauchen	*(to) need, use | needing, using*
Brief (m)	*letter*
Bürgermeister (m)	*mayor*
Café (nt)	*café, coffee shop*
danke	*thanks*
doch	*however, but*
draußen	*outside, outdoors*
eben	*just, now*
ebenfalls	*likewise, also, as well, too*
echt	*genuine, real, genuinely, really*
ehemalig	*former*
eigen	*own, private*
Eindruck (m)	*impression, effect*
einer	*(some)one*
empfehlen	*(to) recommend | recommending*
entdecken	*(to) discover | discovering*
entschied	*(I, she, he, it) decided*
enttäuschen	*(to) disappoint, frustrate | disappointing, frustrating*

		😐	🙂	😎
Erinnerung (f)	*memory, reminder*			
extrem	*extreme, extremely*			
Fenster (nt)	*window*			
Flug (m)	*flight*			
Fluss (m)	*river*			
Frau (f)	*woman, wife, Mrs.*			
frei	*free, available*			
freuen; sich acc. freuen; sich acc. freuen auf + noun	*(to) please, make happy | pleasing, making happy; (to) be happy, pleased | being happy, pleased; (to) look forward to + noun | looking forward to + noun*			
Frühstück (nt)	*breakfast*			
funktionieren	*(to) function, work | functioning, working*			
Gebäude (nt)	*building, buildings*			
gelten	*(to) be valid | being valid*			
(aux) ... gemocht	*liked / (have, has) liked (pp)*			
genau	*exact, exactly, precise, precisely*			
genießen	*(to) enjoy | enjoying*			
genug	*enough*			
(aux) ... geöffnet	*open*			
Glück (nt)	*luck, good luck, fortune, happiness*			
glücklicherweise	*fortunately, luckily*			
Grad (m)	*degree (temperature)*			
günstig	*cheap, favourable, good / cheaply*			
halten; halten ... für + noun	*(to) stop, hold | stopping, holding; (to) think of someone as | thinking of someone as, to keep*			
heiß	*hot*			
herzlich	*cordial, warm, warmly*			
hin	*there*			
historisch	*historical*			
Hotel (nt)	*hotel*			
ideal	*ideal*			
Ihr	*your (formal) (m, nt)*			
Ihre	*your (formal) (f, pl)*			
Information (f)	*information*			
insbesondere	*especially, particularly*			
Insel (f)	*island*			
insgesamt	*in all, altogether, in total, overall*			
inzwischen	*in the meantime, meanwhile*			
irgendein	*some, any (m., nt.)*			
Jahrhundert (nt)	*century*			
kalt	*cold*			
kaputt	*broken, ruined*			
kennenlernen, kennen lernen	*(to) meet (for first time), get to know | meeting (for first time), getting to know*			
klar	*clear, obvious*			
Kraft (f)	*strength, power*			
Küche (f)	*kitchen, cuisine*			
Kultur (f)	*culture*			
Kurs (m)	*course*			
Küste (f)	*coast, shore*			
Lärm (m)	*noise*			
laut	*loud, noisy*			
lecker	*tasty, delicious*			

leider	*unfortunately, sadly*
lief	*(I, she, he, it) ran, walked*
liegen	*(to) lie, be lying (down), be situated | lying, lying (down), being situated*
Linie (f)	*line, route (e.g. bus)*
Luft (f)	*air*
mag	*(I) like / (she, he, it, one) likes*
magst	*(you (sing informal)) like*
Mal (nt)	*time*
Mann (m)	*man, husband, male*
Markt (m)	*market*
Meer (nt)	*sea, ocean*
merken; sich dat. merken	*(to) notice | noticing; to remember | remembering*
Mitarbeiter (m)	*employee, co-worker, colleague*
Museen (pl)	*museums*
natürlich	*natural, naturally, of course, certainly*
nennen; sich acc. nennen	*(to) name, call | naming, calling; (to) be called | being called*
nichts	*nothing*
niemand	*no one (subj)*
niemanden	*no one (obj)*
nur	*only, just*
oben	*above, up there, upstairs*
öffnen	*(to) open | opening*
Ordnung (f)	*order, tidiness*
peinlich	*embarrassing, awkward*

Platz (m)	*place, room, square, seat, pitch (sport)*
plötzlich	*sudden, suddenly*
praktisch	*practical, useful*
probieren	*(to) try, sample | trying, sampling*
Rechnung (f)	*bill, calculation, invoice*
Region (f)	*region, area*
regnen	*(to) rain | raining*
Reise (f)	*journey, trip, voyage*
riesig	*huge, great, tremendous, giant, massive, enormous*
Ruhe (f)	*silence, peace, rest*
ruhig	*quiet, calm*
sauber	*clean*
Schaden (m)	*damage, harm*
schließen	*(to) close, shut | closing, shutting*
Schloss (nt)	*castle*
Schlüssel (m)	*key*
schmutzig	*dirty, filthy*
Schnee (m)	*snow*
schneien	*(to) snow | snowing*
schrecklich	*terrible, awful, dreadful, terribly, awfully, dreadfully*
schwimmen	*(to) swim | swimming*
See (m)	*lake*
See (f)	*sea*
Sei ...!	*Be ...! (sing informal)*
seid	*(you (pl informal)) are | are being*
Seid ...!	*Be ...! (pl informal)*
Seien Sie ...!	*Be ...! (formal)*

Seite (f)	*side, page, hand (on the one/ other hand)*
Sonne (f)	*sun*
sonnig	*sunny*
spazieren	*(to) (go for a) walk, stroll | (going for a) walk, strolling*
Speisekarte (f)	*menu*
stehlen	*(to) steal | stealing*
Strand (m)	*beach, shore*
Straße (f)	*street, road*
Stuhl (m)	*chair*
tauchen	*(to) dive | diving*
Telefon (nt)	*telephone*
teuer	*expensive, dear, costly*
Ticket (nt)	*ticket*
tief	*deep, low*
Tor (nt)	*goal, gate*
Tourist (m)	*tourist*
traditionell	*traditional, traditionally*
Tür (f)	*door*
übrig	*remaining, left, leftover, spare*
unglaublich	*unbelievable, incredible, unbelievably*
unterwegs	*on the way*
Urlaub (m)	*holiday*
vergessen	*(to) forget | forgetting*
verlangen	*(to) request, demand | requesting, demanding*
verlieren; sich verlieren	*(to) lose | losing; (to) get lost (in thought) | getting lost (in thought)*
(aux) ... verloren	*lost*
vermeiden	*(to) avoid | avoiding*

völlig	*completely, absolutely*
Vorschlag (m)	*suggestion, proposal*
Wald (m)	*forest, wood*
warm	*warm*
warten (auf acc. + noun)	*(to) wait (for + noun) | waiting (for + noun)*
was für?	*what sort/type of ...?*
wechseln	*(to) change, exchange (money) | changing, exchanging money*
Weg (m)	*path, way, method*
weit	*far, wide, widely*
Welt (f)	*world*
werdet	*(you (pl informal)) become | are becoming | will (aux)*
Wetter (nt)	*weather*
wieder	*again*
willkommen	*welcome*
Wind (m)	*wind*
WLAN (nt)	*wi-fi*
wohin?	*where ... to?*
würde	*(I, she, he, it) would*
Zeitpunkt (m)	*moment, (point in) time*
Zelt (nt)	*tent*
Zentrum (nt)	*centre, middle*
Zimmer (nt)	*room*
zu Hause	*at home*
zuerst	*first (of all)*
Zukunft (f)	*future*
zurückkommen	*(to) return | returning*
Zustand (m)	*condition, state*

F Revising prepositions with accusative and dative

1 Read this paragraph. Translate the bold words/phrases into English on a separate sheet.

Die **Geschwister** sind in der Schweiz **geboren** und sind **danach** nach Deutschland gekommen. Sie sind **nicht binär** und haben einen **Blog** über **Transgender-Menschen** geschrieben. Sie glauben, wir sollen alle Menschen **akzeptieren**.

G

Some prepositions are always used with either the accusative or the dative case. However **dual-case prepositions** take the **accusative** when there is **movement** involved and the **dative** when there is **no movement**.

accusative prepositions	**dative prepositions**	**dual-case prepositions** (accusative or dative)
für – for *ohne* – without	*mit* – with *nach* – to, after *von* – from, of *aus* – out of, from	*in* – in *vor* – in front of, ago

The **definite** and **indefinite articles** change according to the case that follows the prepositions.

	masc	**fem**	**neut**	**pl**
accusative	d**en** ein**en**	die eine	das ein	die –
dative	d**em** ein**em**	d**er** ein**er**	d**em** ein**em**	den –

Remember that there are short forms of some prepositions and articles.

in das ⟶ *ins*
in dem ⟶ *im*

Movement: *Ich gehe **ins** Sportzentrum.*
No movement: *Ich bin **im** Sportzentrum.*

2 Underline the preposition in each sentence. Then circle the correct form of the article to complete each sentence.

1 Dieser Verein ist in **die** / **der** / **das** Türkei (*f*) und möchte die Welt positiv verändern.

2 Sie arbeiten gemeinsam für **eine** / **einem** / **einer** bessere Welt (*f*).

3 Sie möchten mit **das** / **dem** / **die** Blog (*m*) Personen helfen, die gay sind.

4 Er ist vor **ein** / **einem** / **einen** Jahr (*nt*) nach Deutschland gekommen.

5 Am Montag fahren sie in **die** / **der** / **das** Schweiz (*f*).

Try to work out the meaning of the sentences as you do the exercises. Use the glossary at the end of the module to help you.

3 Underline the preposition in each sentence. Then fill in the correct forms of the definite article ('the').

1 Sie hat von .... Blog (*m*) in .... Schweiz (*f*) gehört.

2 Er steht mit .... Lehrerin (*f*) vor .... Schule (*f*).

3 Sie kommen mit .... Essen (*nt*) aus .... Supermarkt (*m*).

4 Sie macht nach .... Prüfung (*f*) eine Party in .... Garten (*m*).

stehen *to stand*

4 Translate these sentences into German on a separate sheet.

1 She works for the association.

2 She was born in Turkey.

3 She has won many prizes.

4 She came to Austria a year ago.

5 She believes we should accept all people.

Kulturzone Wir verbessern die Welt!

H Using more prepositions with the genitive

H 1 Complete these sentences by translating the words in brackets into German.

1 Er ist .... (*author*) und lebt seit fast 30 Jahren irgendwo in der Schweiz.

2 Es gibt hier viele .... (*refugees*) und er hilft allen.

3 Er hilft Menschen, die von Drogen abhängig sind und hat dabei großen .... (*success*)

4 Er arbeitet für einen guten .... (*purpose*) und hat viele gute Ergebnisse.

5 Man sieht deutlich einen großen .... (*progress*) und er tut alles, damit sie sich in der Schweiz wohlfühlen.

G

H Remember that **some prepositions** in German always take the **genitive** case:

statt	*statt **des** Konflikts*	instead of
trotz	*trotz **des** Fortschritts*	despite
während	*während **der** 60er Jahre*	during
wegen	*wegen sein**er** Arbeit*	because of

	masculine	feminine	neuter	plural
definite article	d**es**	d**er**	d**es**	d**er**
indefinite article	ein**es**	ein**er**	ein**es**	–

The genitive case can also be used to show possession:

*der Zweck **der** Frage*	the purpose of the question
*das Ziel sein**es** Leben**s***	the goal of his life
*die Hälfte **der** Tiere*	half of the animals

H 2 Underline the preposition in each sentence. Then circle the correct form of the article to complete each sentence.

1 Er wurde wegen **seiner** / **seines** Arbeit oft kritisiert.

2 Er hat den Flüchtlingen während **des** / **der** Ferien geholfen.

3 Du solltest „grüne" Kleidung statt **der** / **die** billigen Kleidung kaufen.

4 Trotz **des** / **der** Fortschritts bei den Rechten für Transgender-Menschen gibt es immer noch viele Probleme.

The masculine and neuter nouns are easy to spot: they have an **-s** or **-es** at the end. The others must therefore be feminine or plural.

H 3 Complete each sentence starter with the correct genitive form of the definite article. Then draw lines to match up the sentence halves.

1 Während .... Urlaubs

2 Trotz .... Kritik an seinen Büchern

3 Wegen .... Erfolgs ist er von Österreich

4 Statt .... Autos

a hat man ihn den besten Autor genannt.

b solltest du das Fahrrad nehmen.

c nach Deutschland gezogen.

d hat der Lehrer Kindern geholfen.

H 4 Translate these sentences into German on a separate sheet.

1 My role model is an author who fights for a better society.

2 The purpose of his life is to help all children.

3 Despite his success, he is normal and very nice.

4 I love him because of his great books!

5 We should all help to make the world better.

1 Was ist dir wichtig?

Using verbs followed by prepositions

1 Complete each sentence using a word from the box.

Use the glossary to look up any words that are unfamiliar and try to learn them.

Sorgen	Bildung	Lösung	Freiheit	Sicherheit

1 Wir machen uns große .... um unsere Zukunft.

2 Alle Menschen sollen sich sicher fühlen, deswegen ist für mich die .... für alle Menschen sehr wichtig.

3 Meine .... ist ein wichtiger Aspekt für mich; ich will mich überall frei bewegen.

H 4 Sind die Themen .... und eine sichere Zukunft für deine Generation wichtig?

H 5 Ich hoffe, dass die Diskussion bald ein Ende hat und dass es irgendeine .... für die Umweltprobleme gibt.

G

Many verbs in German are followed by a **preposition**. Remember which case each preposition takes after a verb, and make sure the article that follows agrees with the noun.

sich interessieren ***für*** (+ acc) to be interested **in**
sich freuen ***auf*** (+ acc) to look forward **to**
hoffen ***auf*** (+ acc) to hope **for**
warten ***auf*** (+ acc) to wait **for**
Angst haben ***vor*** (+ dat) to be afraid **of**
diskutieren ***über*** (+ acc) to talk **about**
sprechen ***über*** (+ acc) to speak **about**

To refer to something you have already mentioned, add ***da-*** to the preposition.
Ich interessiere mich ***dafür***. I am interested **in it**.
If the preposition begins with a vowel, add ***dar-***.
Ich freue mich ***darauf***. I am looking forward **to it**.
H Other examples are:
hinter – ***dahinter*** behind it, *neben* – ***daneben*** next to it, *unter* – ***darunter*** underneath it, *zwischen* – ***dazwischen*** in between them

H When asking questions, add ***wo(r)-*** to the preposition.
Wobei *kann ich dir helfen?* **What** can I help you **with**?
Wodurch *hast du es erfahren?* **How/Through what** did you find out about it?
Wogegen *kämpfen sie?* **What** do they fight **against**?
Wohinter *stehst du?* **What** do you stand **behind**?
Wonach *suchst du?* **What** are you looking **for**?
Woneben *ist das?* **What** is that **next to**?
Worauf *wartest du?* **What** are you waiting **for**?
Worunter *ist das?* **What** is that **under**?
Wozwischen *ist das?* **What** is that **between**?

2 Circle the correct word to complete each sentence.

1 Er spricht im Fernsehen **darauf / darüber**.

2 Dieser große Hund? Ja, ich habe Angst **darauf / davor**!

3 Ich freue mich **dafür / darauf**, dass ich nächste Woche Ferien habe.

4 Ich hoffe **dafür / darauf**, dass alle Menschen dieselben Freiheiten haben.

H 5 Ich warte **dafür / darauf**, dass ich endlich studieren kann.

H 6 Ich interessiere mich **dafür / darauf**, was in der Welt passiert.

3 Underline the preposition in each question. Then complete each answer using a word from the box.

davon   daraus   darin   davor   darüber   darauf

1 Hoffst du auf eine gute Zukunft? *Ja, ich hoffe ....*

2 Hast du von diesem Artikel gehört? *Ja, ich habe .... gehört.*

H 3 Wovor hast du Angst? *Ich habe Angst ...., dass es Krieg gibt.*

H 4 Habt ihr über den Konflikt gesprochen? *Ja, wir haben .... gesprochen.*

H 5 Woraus kann man etwas lernen? *Man kann .... etwas lernen, dass man Umweltprobleme löst.*

H 6 Worin siehst du einen Sinn? *Ich sehe .... einen Sinn, dass die Menschen über die Probleme sprechen.*

H **4 Match up the questions with their answers. Write the correct letter.**

1 Woran denkst du? ....

2 Wovon hast du gehört? ....

3 Womit bist du allgemein zufrieden? ....

4 Wozu braucht ihr das Internet? ....

5 Worüber habt ihr diskutiert? ....

6 Wofür kämpft ihr? ....

7 Worum geht es hier? ....

a Wir brauchen das Internet dazu, um uns über die aktuelle Situation zu informieren.

b Ich denke daran, dass ich heute irgendwann noch meine Hausaufgaben machen muss.

c Wir haben darüber diskutiert, wie man irgendetwas für die Umwelt tun kann.

d Es geht darum, über dieses Thema zu sprechen und das Gute zu erkennen.

e Wir kämpfen dafür, dass sich alle Menschen sicher fühlen können.

f Ich habe davon gehört, dass viele Menschen auf der Welt an Hunger leiden.

g Ich bin allgemein damit zufrieden, dass ich ein gutes Leben habe.

F **5 Translate these sentences into German on a separate sheet.**

1 My freedom is very important to me.

2 I am afraid of the exams.

3 I hope for a good future for me and my friends.

4 I am interested in it.

5 I'm looking forward to my studies.

Remember, there are two ways to say how important something is to someone:
Für mich *ist die Gesundheit wichtig. / Die Gesundheit ist wichtig für mich.*
Mir *ist die Gesundheit wichtig. / Die Gesundheit ist mir wichtig.*

H **6 Translate these sentences into English on a separate sheet.**

1 Für mich ist die Bildung sehr wichtig.

2 Mein Vorbild kämpft dafür, dass alle Menschen frei sein sollen.

3 Die Entwicklung ist ein wichtiger Aspekt davon.

4 Das Wichtigste ist, dass alle Menschen die gleichen Rechte haben sollen.

5 Ich mache mir große Sorgen darum und möchte darüber sprechen.

Adjectives can be used to create neuter nouns by adding a capital letter and **-e**.
gut: ***Das Gute*** *ist* ... The good thing is ...
Superlative forms can also be used by adding **-ste**.
schlimm: ***Das Schlimmste*** *daran ist* ... The worst thing about it is ...

2 Unser armer Planet

Revising compound nouns

1 Unjumble the letters to rewrite the nouns correctly. Add the definite article *der, die, das* and translate them into English.

1 laGs ....

2 aBmu ....

3 Ghrefa ....

4 ltUemw ....

5 tempuTerar ....

6 ülMl ....

H 7 lmKia ....

2 Complete each sentence using a verb from the box.

benutzen	kaufen	sammeln	fahren
brauchen	trennen	wegwerfen	schützen

1 Ich sorge mich um die armen Tiere, die in Gefahr sind. Wir müssen sie retten und ....

2 Man soll das Licht nur dann ...., wenn es nötig ist, und Energie sparen.

3 Man soll Glasflaschen .... und nicht ....

H 4 Wenige Deutsche .... Elektroautos.

H 5 Alle Menschen .... reine Luft und sauberes Wasser.

H 6 Wir sollen im Supermarkt umweltfreundliche Produkte ....

H 7 Man muss den Müll ....

Try to work out the meaning of the sentences as you do the exercises. Use the glossary to look up any unfamiliar words and try to learn them.

3 Draw lines to match up the compound noun halves.

1 das Trink — **a** problem

2 das Umwelt — **b** auto

3 die Klein — **c** blatt

4 das Baum — **d** stadt

H 5 das Elektro — **e** teil

H 6 das Gegen — **f** wasser

4 Write the correct definite article (*der, die* or *das*) for each compound noun. Then translate the nouns into English.

1 Verkehrsmittel ....

2 Glasflasche ....

G

Remember that **compound nouns** can be formed from:

- two nouns:

Musik + Instrument → *das Musikinstrument*

- a verb stem and a noun:

laufen + Schuhe → *die Laufschuhe*

- an adjective and a noun:

groß + Stadt → *die Großstadt*

When the first noun ends in a consonant, it is common to add an **-s-** to link the words:

der Einkauf (from *einkaufen*)
+ das Zentrum → *das Einkauf**s**zentrum*

The gender of a compound noun will always be determined by the gender of the final noun in the word.

In the same way as compound nouns, other **compound words** such as **adjectives** can be formed:

die Umwelt + freundlich →
umweltfreundlich environmentally friendly

3 Gesundheitssystem ....

4 Naturschutz ....

5 Fahrrad ....

H 6 Klimawandel ....

H 5 Underline the compound noun in each sentence.

1 Ich habe bewusst angefangen, Glasflaschen zu sammeln und nicht wegzuwerfen.

2 Ich möchte mich mehr über den Klimaschutz und neue Energien informieren.

3 Die Bundesregierung hilft Flüchtlingen, denn ihnen droht Gefahr.

4 Ein sehr schlimmes Problem ist, dass die Tiere sterben und viele Tierarten verschwinden.

5 Die Umweltstudie sagt, dass in der Vergangenheit viele Tiere gestorben sind.

If you encounter unknown words, use a dictionary to translate them. Look out for cognates (words that are the same or similar in both languages) and similarities between nouns and adjectives.

F 6 Translate these sentences into English.

1 Extremes Wetter ist ein großes Umweltproblem.

....

2 In diesem Blog kann man viel über den Naturschutz lesen.

....

3 Alle Länder sollen ein gutes Gesundheitssystem haben.

....

4 Fahrräder sind saubere Verkehrsmittel.

....

5 Viele Menschen haben kein sauberes Trinkwasser und das ist gefährlich.

....

H 7 Translate these sentences into German.

1 In my opinion, the worst problem is the dirty air.

....

2 I think everyone should go by bicycle.

....

3 It's very important to buy environmentally friendly products.

....

4 We also need consciously to separate our rubbish.

....

5 Have you already started to save the climate?

....

3 Jeder kann was tun!

- Using *wollen* (to want to)
- Using verbs in three time frames

1 Circle the odd one out.

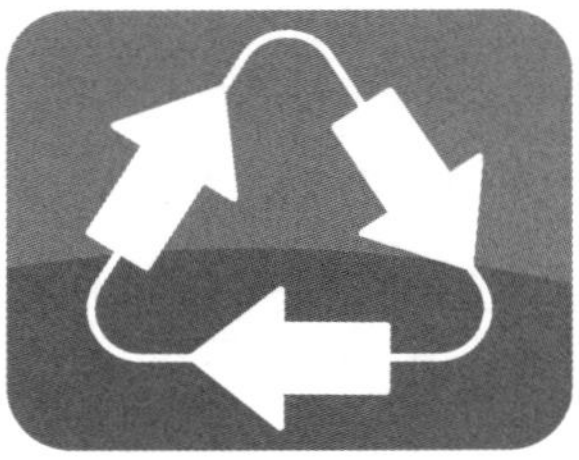

1 verlassen / umweltfreundlich / sammeln / recyceln

2 Papier / Blog / Wasser / Glas

3 manchmal / immer / retten / ab und zu

4 anrufen / wegwerfen / anfangen / kaufen

H 5 teilnehmen / verwenden / verantwortlich / trennen

2 Underline the verb(s) in each sentence. Write down the infinitive and translate it into English.

1 Wir sparen jeden Tag Wasser. ....

2 Ich sammle ab und zu leere Glasflaschen. ....

3 Er recycelt oft Papier, denn Recycling ist wichtig! ....

4 Ich benutze das Licht nur wenn nötig. ....

H 5 Leider trennt meine Tante weder Flaschen noch Zeitungen.

....

H 6 In diesem Projekt hat man schon seit 1974 getrennten Müll gehabt!

....

H 7 Du musst aufhören, immer so viel neue Kleidung zu kaufen.

....

> Some sentences may have more than one verb. If there are unknown verbs, use a dictionary or the glossary to translate them.

G

Use ***wollen*** + infinitive to express what people want to do.

ich will	wir wollen
du willst	ihr wollt
er/sie/es/man will	Sie/sie wollen

With **modal verbs**, the second verb (the infinitive) must go to the end of the sentence.

*Wir **wollen** die Umwelt schützen.*

We **want to** protect the environment.

Don't confuse *wollen* (want to) with *werden* (will). To express the future, use *werden* + infinitive.

*Wir **werden** die Umwelt schützen.*

We **will** protect the environment.

H The modal verb **wollen** can also be used with a noun on its own:

*Wir **wollen** keine Konflikte.*

We don't **want** conflicts.

3 Complete these German translations.

1 I want to save water more often. *Ich* .... *öfter Wasser* ....

2 Do you want to buy fewer new clothes? .... *ihr weniger neue Kleidung* ....?

3 We want to recycle more paper. *Wir* .... *mehr Papier* ....

4 Mrs Schmidt, do you want to use the light only when it is necessary? *Frau Schmidt,* .... *Sie das Licht nur verwenden, wenn es nötig ist?*

5 Mark, do you want to go to school on foot or go by car? *Mark,* .... *du zu Fuß zur Schule* .... *oder mit dem Auto* ....?

H 6 The people want more glass bottles. *Die Menschen* .... *mehr Glasflaschen.*

4 Complete these sentences with the correct form of the verb in brackets in German.

1 Ich werde jeden Tag Papier .... (*recycle*)

2 Sie wollen jetzt öfter mit dem Fahrrad zur Schule .... (*drive, go*)

3 Hast du schon wieder neue Kleidung ....? (*buy*)

4 .... du Glasflaschen? (*collect*)

5 Ich werde nie wieder Papier .... (*throw away*)

H 6 Marie und Paul brauchen das Licht nicht mehr, wenn sie das Haus .... haben. (*leave*)

G

Understanding and using three time frames in your work will help you to target higher grades.

Present: *Ich* ***kaufe*** *umweltfreundliche Produkte.*

Past: *Ich* ***habe*** *umweltfreundliche Produkte* ***gekauft****.*

Future: *Ich* ***werde*** *umweltfreundliche Produkte* ***kaufen****.*

Remember where the prefix goes on separable verbs in the present tense. Also remember where **-ge-** goes in the past (perfect) tense.

Present: *Ich* ***rufe*** *meine Mutter* ***an****.*

Past: *Ich* ***habe*** *meine Mutter* ***angerufen****.*

Future: *Ich* ***werde*** *meine Mutter* ***anrufen****.*

H 5 Underline the verb(s) in each sentence and write down the tense each sentence is in. Then, on a separate sheet, rewrite the sentence in the tense indicated in brackets.

1 Ich kaufe immer umweltfreundliche Produkte und das ist eine gute Tat für die Umwelt. .... (*past*)

2 Ich war Mitglied in einer Organisation für Klimaschutz. .... (*future*)

3 Wir sind alle für die Umwelt verantwortlich. .... (*future*)

4 Wir tragen heute alle die Verantwortung für unsere Zukunft. .... (*past*)

5 Sie werden einen Versuch machen und umweltfreundliche Produkte entwickeln. .... (*present*)

F 6 Translate these sentences into German.

1 I'm usually very environmentally friendly. ....

2 He uses very little light. ....

3 She will go by bike more often. ....

4 We collected paper every day. ....

5 You want to do more for the environment in the future. ....

H 7 Translate these sentences into English on a separate sheet.

1 Willst du für die Umwelt verantwortlich sein und gegen den Klimawandel kämpfen?

2 Du kannst Mitglied in einer Organisation für Umweltschutz werden.

3 In diesem Projekt kann jeder irgendetwas tun, um der Natur zu helfen.

4 Wir wollen an verschiedenen Veranstaltungen teilnehmen und in der Gesellschaft aktiv sein.

5 Ihr könnt auch Geld sammeln, Veranstaltungen organisieren und dadurch der Umwelt helfen.

4 Wir wollen eine bessere Welt!

- Using *man*
- Using the conditional of *sollen*

1 Draw lines to match up the German words with their English translations.

1	die Europäische Union	a	truth
2	die Erde	b	citizen
H 3	die Wahrheit	c	star
H 4	der Bürger / die Bürgerin	d	Earth
H 5	der Stern	e	EU

2 Complete each section using a word from the box.

zahlen leben europäische dürfen praktisch reisen

1 Die EU hat 27 .... Länder.

2 Die Menschen können oft frei in die EU-Mitgliedsländer ....

3 Sie können normalerweise auch mit dem Euro ...., was sehr .... ist.

4 Sie .... auch in anderen Ländern .... und arbeiten.

G

Man can be translated as 'you', 'people (in general)', 'they' or occasionally 'one'. Remember when using **modal verbs** that the second verb in the sentence will be in the infinitive and it will be at the end of the clause.

Man ***kann*** *Geld sammeln.*
Man ***will*** *abnehmen.*
Man ***soll*** *Kindern helfen.*
Man ***darf*** *in die Schule gehen.*
H *Man* ***muss*** *die Situation ändern.*

G

H ***sollte-*** is the conditional form of *sollen* and means 'should'. Just as in the present tense, the conditional form of modal verbs also sends the second verb (the infinitive) to the end of the clause.

Man ***sollte*** *alle Menschen akzeptieren.*
You/They/One **should** accept all human beings.
Ich ***sollte*** *selbstverständlich für die Einführung und Entwicklung neuer Technologien kämpfen.*
I **should** obviously fight for the introduction and development of new technologies.

*ich soll**te***	*wir soll**ten***
*du soll**test***	*ihr soll**tet***
*er/sie/es/man soll**te***	*Sie/sie soll**ten***

3 Rewrite each sentence, putting the words into the correct order.

1 Tiere die Man retten will ....

2 Schule Man zu kann Fuß zur gehen ....

3 Papier und Man sammeln recyceln soll ....

4 Man akzeptieren Menschen muss alle ....

5 Quelle das darf aus trinken Wasser Man der ....

4 Rewrite these sentences using *man*.

die Quelle	*source*

1 Viele Menschen können in der EU wählen. ....

2 Die Teilnehmer wollen den Menschen offenbar immer irgendwie helfen.

....

3 In der EU dürfen die Menschen oft frei reisen.

....

H 4 Die Bürger müssen die Wahrheit über den Konflikt erfahren, um das Land wieder aufbauen zu können.

....

H 5 Große internationale Unternehmen sollten menschlich sein und feststellen, wo es brennt, und dann Hilfe anbieten.

....

wo es brennt literally means 'where it is burning'. It is an idiom to express that there is a problem or a crisis.

H **5 Circle the correct form of *sollte-* to complete each sentence.**

1 Die EU **sollte** / **sollten** / **solltest** sich um den Streit zwischen Ländern kümmern.

2 Sie **solltest** / **sollten** / **solltet** anfangen, die Situation zu verbessern, um eine Krise zu vermeiden.

3 Man **sollte** / **solltet** / **sollten** dazu erst eine Umfrage fordern.

4 Die Menschen **sollte** / **solltet** / **sollten** nicht auf Tiere schießen und sie töten.

5 Die Regierung **sollten** / **solltest** / **sollte** das durch ein Gesetz verbieten.

F **6 Translate these sentences into English.**

1 Du hilfst Tieren in Gefahr. ....

2 Man kann den armen Ländern helfen. ....

3 Wir sollen alle Religionen akzeptieren. ....

4 Man darf in der EU fast überall frei reisen. ....

5 Man muss über Probleme diskutieren. ....

H **7 Translate these sentences into German.**

Remember that in German the preposition *seit* ('since') is used with the present tense.

1 The EU has only existed since 1993.

....

2 In the EU there are 27 countries and 24 languages.

....

3 Citizens who are living in a member state can normally travel freely.

....

4 You can also pay with the euro in many European countries.

....

5 Therefore, you should absolutely travel to Europe!

....

5 Dialog ist wichtig!

Using phrases of debating

1 Draw lines to match up the English words with their German translations.

1 risk	**a** das Wort
2 vegan	**b** der Vegetarier / die Vegetarierin
3 vegetarian	**c** das Fleisch
4 communication	**d** die Alternative
5 word	**e** der Veganer/ die Veganerin
6 meat	**f** die Kommunikation
H 7 alternative	**g** das Risiko

sieht ist muss
isst scheint werfen

2 Complete each sentence using a verb from the box.

1 Wenn es regnet und die Sonne nicht ...., funktioniert die Sache nicht.

2 Welche Risiken gibt es, wenn man kein Fleisch ....?

3 Sie .... nie Essen weg, sie essen es am nächsten Tag.

H 4 Wenn man hinausgeht, ... man, dass die Windenergie funktioniert.

H 5 Ich .... dich warnen: Das ist nicht gut für die Umwelt und zerstört sie.

H 6 Die Menschen verschmutzen die Luft und das .... eine Ursache für den Klimawandel.

Use these phrases for **spoken debates**:

Das stimmt!	That is correct!
Du hast Recht ...	You are right ...
Meiner Meinung nach ...	In my opinion ...
Ich meine, dass ...	I think / have an opinion that ...
Ich denke/glaube/finde, dass ...	I think/believe/find that ...
H *Ich bin der Meinung, dass ...*	I'm of the opinion that ...
H *Im Gegenteil, ...*	On the contrary / Quite the opposite ...
H *Ich beweise (trotzdem) ...*	I prove (nevertheless) ...
H *Ich bin (übrigens) davon überzeugt, dass ...*	I am (by the way) convinced that ...
H *Du überzeugst mich, dass ...*	You convince me that ...

3 Separate out the words and write out the sentences.

1 WoherwissenSiedas? ....

2 Dasstimmt,Windenergieistsehrsauber. ....

3 DuhastRecht,aberneueEnergienkostenvielGeld.

....

4 Ichfinde,dassnurGemüseessenlangweiligist.

....

5 Ichdenke,dassesinmeinemLandvieleUmweltproblemegibt.

....

6 MeinerMeinungnachistesnichtgutfürdieGesundheit,wennmanzuvielFleischisst.

....

4 Rewrite the second part of each sentence, putting the words into the correct order.

1 Du hast Recht, ... ich werde versuchen das ....

2 Ich glaube, dass ... Gefühle Tiere auch haben ....

3 Meiner Meinung nach ist Fleisch lecker, aber ... gesünder Gemüse ist ....

H 4 Das stimmt, aber ... Vegetarier gibt wenige oft Alternativen für es ....

H 5 Das ist zwar wahr, aber ... offensichtlich Gemüse mir nicht schmeckt ....

H 5 Translate the underlined German verbs into English using words from the box.

is	are lacking	
prevent	cause	grow

1 Ich bin davon überzeugt, dass schmutzige Luft und schmutziges Wasser den Klimawandel <u>verursachen</u>. ....

2 Ich sage, dass in den Restaurants Alternativen für Vegetarier und Veganer <u>fehlen</u>. ....

3 Ich bin der Meinung, dass man den Klimawandel auf diese Weise <u>verhindern</u> kann. ....

4 Ich glaube fest daran, dass die Wirtschaft am Klimawandel Schuld <u>ist</u>. ....

5 Hast du gewusst, dass hier so wenige Bäume <u>wachsen</u>? ....

F 6 Translate these sentences into German.

Start with *Man*.

1 We must protect nature. ....

2 Too much meat is not good for the environment. ....

3 I believe that green energy works. ....

4 In my opinion, vegetarians live more healthily. ....

5 Yes, you're right, but I also think that there are many vegetarians today. ....

H 7 Translate these sentences into English on a separate sheet.

1 Die Krise ist zwar nicht so schlimm, aber wir müssen trotzdem irgendeine Lösung finden.

2 Meiner Meinung nach sollte die Bundesregierung mehr gegen den Klimawandel kämpfen.

3 Ich finde übrigens, dass diese Umfrage sehr nützlich war.

4 Du hast Recht: Wir sind alle für eine saubere Umwelt verantwortlich.

5 Du hast mich überzeugt und ich weiß, ich kann das schaffen!

Glossary

bold = this word will appear in Higher exams only

abhängig	*dependent, addicted*
abnehmen	*(to) lose weight, decrease, reduce*
aktuell	*current, up-to-date, topical*
allgemein	*general*
Alternative (f)	*alternative*
ändern	*(to) change, alter*
anfangen	*(to) start | starting*
Angst (f)	*fear, anxiety*
arm	*poor*
Art (f)	*type, kind, sort*
Aspekt (m)	*aspect*
aufbauen	*(to) build up, construct*
aufhören	*(to) stop*
Baum (m)	*tree*
beweisen	*(to) prove, demonstrate*
bewusst	*conscious, aware*
Bildung (f)	*education, learning, creation, formation*
Blatt (nt)	*sheet, leaf*
Blog (m) (nt)	*blog*
brennen	*(to) burn*
Bundesregierung (f)	*federal government*
Bürger (m)	*citizen (m)*
dabei	with it, there
dadurch	*through it, as a result, as a consequence*
dahinter	*behind it*
damit (conj)	*so that*
damit (pron)	*with it*
danach (adv)	*afterwards*
danach (pron)	***after it**, afterwards*
daneben	*next to it, beside it*
daran, dran	*on it, at it, in the process of it*
darauf, drauf	*on it, onto it, at it, to it*
daraus	*out of it, from it*
darin, drin, drinnen	*in it, in there, inside*
darüber, drüber	*above/about it*
darum	*around it, therefore*
darunter	*under it, underneath*
das Gute	*the good thing*
davon	*from it, about it*
davor	*before (it), in front of it*
dazwischen	*in between, between/ among (them)*
derselbe, dieselbe, dasselbe	*the same (one/s)*
deswegen	therefore, for this reason
deutlich	*clear, clearly*
der Deutsche (m), (ein) Deutscher	*(the) German, (a) German (m)*
die, eine Deutsche (f)	*(the, a) German (f)*
Deutsche (pl), die Deutschen	*Germans, (the) Germans (pl)*
Diskussion (f)	*discussion, debate*
diskutieren (über acc. + noun)	*(to) discuss (+ noun) | discussing*
drohen	*(to) threaten*
Einführung (f)	*introduction*
Elektroauto (nt)	*electric car/ vehicle*

entwickeln	*(to) develop*
Entwicklung (f)	*development*
Erde (f)	*earth, ground, soil, world*
Erfolg (m)	*success*
Ergebnis (nt)	*result, outcome*
erst	*first, only, not until*
europäisch	*European*
existieren	*(to) exist*
fehlen	*(to) lack, be missing/absent lacking, being missing/absent*
feststellen	*(to) establish, detect, determine, realise*
Flasche (f)	*bottle*
Fleisch (nt)	*meat, flesh*
Flüchtling (m)	*refugee*
fordern	*(to) demand, claim*
Fortschritt (m)	*progress*
Freiheit (f)	*freedom*
gay	*gay*
geboren	*born*
Gefahr (f)	*danger, risk, threat*
gefährlich	*dangerous, risky*
Gefühl (nt)	*feeling*
Gegenteil (nt)	*opposite*
gemeinsam	*(in) common, mutual, joint*
(aux) ... genannt	*named / named (pp)*
Generation (f)	*generation*
(aux) ... gestorben	*died*
Gesetz (nt)	*law*
getrennt	*separated*
(aux) ... gewusst	*knew / known (pp)*
Glas (nt)	*glass*
Hälfte (f)	*half*
heute	*today*
hinaus	*out, beyond*
informieren; sich (acc.) informieren über (+ noun)	*(to) inform; (to) find out about (+ noun)*
international	*international*
Internet (nt)	*internet*
irgendeine	*some, any (f)*
irgendetwas, irgendwas	*something, anything*
irgendwann	*sometime, some day*
irgendwie	*somehow*
irgendwo	*somewhere*
Klima (f)	*climate*
Klimawandel (m)	*climate change*
Kommunikation (f)	*communication*
Konflikt (m)	*conflict, dispute*
Krieg (m)	*war*
Krise (f)	*crisis*
kritisieren	*(to) criticise*
leer	*empty*
leiden (an dat. + noun) (unter dat. + noun)	*(to) suffer (from + noun) (as a result of + noun) | suffering*
Licht (nt)	*light*
Lösung (f)	*solution, answer*
meinen	*(to) think, have an opinion | thinking, having an opinion*
menschlich	*human*
Mitglied (nt)	*member*
Mittel (nt)	*means, average*
Müll (m)	*rubbish, waste, litter*
nicht binär, nichtbinär	*non-binary*
offenbar	*apparent(ly), obvious(ly)*
offensichtlich	*obvious(ly)*

Organisation (f)	*organisation*
Papier (nt)	*paper*
Produkt (nt)	*product*
Projekt (nt)	*project*
Quelle (f)	*source, spring*
recyceln	*(to) recycle | recycling*
Recycling (nt)	*recycling*
Regierung (f)	*rule, government*
rein	*pure, clear, clean, total(ly)*
retten	*(to) save, rescue | saving, rescuing*
Risiken (pl)	*risks, hazards, dangers*
Risiko (nt)	*risk, hazard, danger*
Sache (f)	*thing, matter*
sammeln	*(to) collect, gather | collecting, gathering*
scheinen	*(to) seem, appear, shine | seeming, appearing, shining*
schießen (auf acc. + noun)	*(to) shoot (at + noun); kick (ball)*
schlimm	*bad, serious*
schmecken	*(to) taste*
Schuld (f)	*guilt, blame, debt*
schützen (vor dat. + noun)	*(to) protect (from + noun) | protecting (from + noun)*
selbstverständlich	*natural(ly), self-evident(ly), obvious(ly)*
sich kümmern um (+ noun)	*(to) take care of (+ noun), be concerned about (+) noun | taking care of, being concerned about*
Sicherheit (f)	*security, safety, certainty*
sollte	*(I, she, he, it, one) was supposed to / **should (conditional)***
solltest	*(you (sing informal)) were supposed to / **should (conditional)***
Sorge (f)	*worry, care*
sorgen	*(to) care, (to) worry | caring, worrying*
sparen	*(to) save | saving*
sterben (an dat. + noun)	*(to) die (from + noun) | dying (from + noun)*
Stern (m)	*star*
stimmen; stimmen für + noun	*(to) be correct | being correct; (to) vote for + noun | voting for (+ noun)*
Streit (m)	*argument, fight, dispute*
Studie (f)	*study, survey*
Tat (f)	*deed, action*
teilnehmen (an dat. + noun)	*(to) take part (in + noun) | taking part (in + noun)*
Teilnehmer (m)	*participant, entrant*
Temperatur (f)	*temperature*
Thema (nt)	*topic, theme*
Themen (pl)	*topics, themes*
Tier (nt)	*animal*
töten	*(to) kill | killing*
trans(gender)	*transgender*
trennen	*(to) separate*
trotz	*in spite of*
trotzdem	*nevertheless*
überzeugen	*(to) convince, persuade*

übrigens	*by the way*			
Umfrage (f)	*survey*			
Umwelt (f)	*environment*			
Ursache (f)	*cause, reason*			
Veganer(in) (m/f)	*vegan*			
Vegetarier(in) (m/f)	*vegetarian*			
verändern	*(to) change / changing*			
verantwortlich	*responsible, in charge*			
Verantwortung (f)	*responsibility*			
verbessern	*(to) improve, correct / improving, correcting*			
verbieten	*(to) forbid, prohibit, ban*			
Vergangenheit (f)	*past*			
verhindern	*(to) prevent*			
verlassen	*(to) leave / leaving*			
verschmutzen	*(to) pollute, contaminate / polluting, contaminating*			
verschwinden	*(to) disappear / disappearing*			
Versuch (m)	*attempt, experiment*			
versuchen	*(to) try / trying*			
verursachen	*(to) cause*			
verwenden	*(to) use*			
wachsen	*(to) grow, increase*			
wahr	*true, real, genuine*			
während	*during, while, whereas*			
Wahrheit (f)	*truth*			
warnen (vor dat. + noun)	*(to) warn (of/ about + noun)*			
weder ... noch	*neither ... nor*			
weg	*gone, vanished, away*			
wegen	*because of*			
Weise (f)	*way, manner*			
wenige	*few*			
werfen	*(to) throw / throwing*			
Wirtschaft (f)	*economy, commerce*			
wobei	*with which, in the process of / during which*			
wodurch	*how, through which, as a result of which*			
wofür	*for what*			
wogegen	*against what, whereas*			
woher?	*where ... from?*			
wohinter	*behind what*			
womit	*with which*			
wonach	*what ... for, what ... of*			
woneben	*next to what, beside what*			
woran	*on/at what*			
worauf	*on/at what*			
woraus	*from what/ which*			
worin	*in(to) what*			
Wort (nt)	*word*			
worüber	*what about*			
worum	*about what*			
worunter	*under which, under what*			
wovon	*from/about what*			
wovor	*what ... of, what ... in front of*			
wozu	*on/onto/at/to what*			
wozwischen	*between what/ which things*			
zerstören	*(to) destroy, ruin / destroying, ruining*			
zufrieden	*satisfied, happy, content*			
zwar	*admittedly, to be precise, indeed*			
Zweck (m)	*purpose, aim*			

Kulturzone Ich will helfen

F Using *möchten* and *wollen*

1 Complete the text using the nouns in the box.

Ideen Arbeitsalltag Prozent Erfahrungen Prüfungen

Wie entscheide ich mich und was mache ich nach der Schule? Ich weiß noch nicht hundert **1** .... Wie wird meine Zukunft nach den **2** .... aussehen? Ich habe so einige **3** .... Meine Eltern wollen, dass ich ein Studium mache, aber ich möchte erst einige **4** .... sammeln. Wie sieht ein **5** .... aus? Das möchte ich selbst sehen.

Try to work out the meaning of the sentences as you do the exercises. Don't be disheartened if you don't know the words yet! Use the glossary at the end of the module to help you.

G

Use the following constructions when you want to say what you **would like to do** or **want to do**:
Ich möchte + infinitive (I would like to …)
Ich will + infinitive (I want to …, **not** 'I will'!)

möchten (*would like to*)	**wollen** (*want to*)
ich möchte	ich will
du möchtest	du willst
er/sie/es/man möchte	er/sie/es/man will
wir möchten	wir wollen
ihr möchtet	ihr wollt
Sie möchten	Sie wollen
sie möchten	sie wollen

2 Complete each sentence using a modal verb from the box.

möchten will möchtest wollt

1 Silvia und Malik, was .... ihr nach den Prüfungen machen?
2 Herr Schiller, ... Sie weiter der Umwelt helfen?
3 Katharina, ... du im Krankenhaus arbeiten?
4 Was .... Maria nach der Schule machen?

3 Complete these sentences with the correct form of the modal verb in brackets, in German.

1 Ich .... mit älteren Menschen arbeiten, genauso wie meine Schwester. (*want*)
2 Robin .... mit Katzen arbeiten, die in Gefahr sind und Hilfe brauchen. (*would like*)
3 .... ihr erst einen Beruf lernen und danach vielleicht studieren? (*would like*)
4 .... du einen Job haben und 1 200 Euro im Monat verdienen? (*want*)
5 Ich .... nicht sitzen bleiben und das Jahr wiederholen, deshalb lerne ich viel. (*would like*)

4 Translate these sentences into German on a separate sheet.

1 Should I do studies?
2 I want to learn practical things.
3 After school we want to do an interesting job.
4 My girlfriend would like to work with people in the future.
5 Would you like to experience a working day?

H 1 Complete each sentence using a word from the box.

Vorstellung Entscheidung weitere unbedingt hoffentlich Gelegenheit

1 Was man nach den Prüfungen machen will, ist eine schwierige ....

2 Nach der Schule will ich .... gleich auf die Universität gehen.

3 Ich möchte etwas Gutes tun und .... auch praktische Dinge lernen.

4 Man hat die ...., wertvolle Kenntnisse und Erfahrungen zu sammeln.

5 Ich habe jetzt eine bessere ...., was ich nach der Schule machen will.

6 Ich weiß, dass ich ohne eine .... Ausbildung keinen guten Job finden werde.

G

H You need to use **zu** with an <u>infinitive</u> after some verbs:

hoffen to hope

planen to plan

(sich) entscheiden to decide

***vor**haben* to intend

***Ich hoffe**, in der Zukunft langfristig im Umweltschutz **zu** <u>arbeiten</u>.*

***Ich habe vor**, ein freiwilliges Jahr **zu** <u>machen</u>.*

Some other constructions also follow the same pattern:

bereit sein, ... zu ...	to be ready / prepared to ...
die Gelegenheit haben, ... zu ...	to have the opportunity to ...
es ist (nicht) leicht, ... zu ...	it is (not) easy to ...
Lust haben, ... zu ...	to feel like doing something
statt ... zu ...	instead of ...

***Es ist nicht leicht**, heraus**zu**<u>finden</u>, was man werden möchte.*

***Ich habe Lust**, neue Länder <u>kennen</u>**zu**<u>lernen</u>.* (separable verb!)

***Statt** mir einen Job **zu** <u>suchen</u>, ...*

Modal verbs in German do **not** use **zu** before the infinitive.

H 2 Rewrite these sentences using *zu* + infinitive on a separate sheet. Start your sentences with the phrases in brackets.

1 Ich will etwas Gutes für die Gesellschaft leisten. (*Ich habe vor, ...*)

2 Ich möchte alte und kranke Menschen pflegen. (*Ich habe entschieden, ...*)

3 Ich möchte auf jeden Fall verschiedene Sachen erleben. (*Ich habe Lust, ...*)

4 Ich möchte nicht sofort auf die Universität gehen, sondern erst ein sogenanntes freiwilliges Jahr machen. (*Statt sofort auf die Universität ...*)

H 3 Rewrite each pair of sentences as one sentence using *zu* + infinitive. Write on a separate sheet.

1 Ich hoffe. Ich studiere später. Ich hoffe, später zu studieren. ....

2 Außerdem bin ich bereit. Ich lerne neue Dinge.

3 Man hat die Gelegenheit. Man hilft anderen Menschen.

4 Es ist nicht leicht. Ich spreche in einem Satz über die Zukunft.

H 4 Translate these sentences into German on a separate sheet.

1 I have decided to do a voluntary year after school.

2 He is ready to do something good for society and care for sick children.

3 You have the opportunity to learn new things.

4 We hope to gain a lot of different experiences.

5 I plan to work in a hospital.

Use the verb meaning '(to) collect, gather'.

1 Was wirst du nach deinen Prüfungen machen?

Using reflexive verbs

1 Unjumble the letters to rewrite the words correctly. Then translate them into English.

1 mFair ....
2 lGde ....
3 prGäesch ....
4 rLeerh ....
H 5 erhLe ....
H 6 esObufter ....

2 Complete each sentence using a word from the box.

1 Ich möchte auf die Universität gehen und da .... sein.
2 Ich denke, ich werde mir eine Stelle suchen, denn ich will .... Geld verdienen.
3 Ich hoffe, dass ich eine .... ohne zu viel Arbeit finde!
H 4 Ich bin mir noch nicht ...., was ich nach den Prüfungen tun werde.
H 5 Ich hoffe auf gute ...., damit ich in großen Firmen Arbeit suchen kann.

Noten
gleich
sicher
Student
Ausbildung

3 Circle the correct reflexive pronoun to complete each sentence.

1 Ich freue **mich** / **dich** / **sich** auf die vielen Möglichkeiten.
2 Wir entscheiden **sich** / **mich** / **uns** für die Universität.
3 Sie verstehen **sich** / **uns** / **euch** wahrscheinlich sehr gut mit ihren Eltern.
4 Du musst **sich** / **dich** / **euch** entscheiden.

G

Reflexive verbs are used with a pronoun which usually goes straight after the verb.

ich interessiere ***mich***	*wir interessieren* ***uns***
du interessierst ***dich***	*ihr interessiert* ***euch***
er/sie/es/man interessiert ***sich***	*Sie/sie interessieren* ***sich***

Ich interessiere ***mich*** *für die Umwelt.* I am interested in the environment.

After subordinating conjunctions like ***dass*** (that) and ***weil*** (because), the reflexive pronoun comes after the subject (e.g. *ich, wir*) and the verb goes to the end of the clause.

Ich entscheide ***mich*** *für eine Arbeit mit Tieren,* ***weil*** *ich* ***mich*** *für die Umwelt interessiere.*

I decide to work with animals because I'm interested in the environment.

4 Rewrite each sentence, putting the words into the correct order.

1 Interessiert euch Computer? ihr für
....
2 Ich meinen Freunden. sehr mich mit verstehe gut
....
3 Wir bei unseren entschuldigen uns Eltern
....
H 4 Sie ihrem sich mit unterhalten Arbeitgeber
....
H 5 Ich an Tisch. mich setze den ....
H 6 Sie Bett. sich ins legen ....
H 7 Ich Job. einen mir tollen wünsche ....

G

Reflexive pronouns can be in the **accusative** or the **dative** case.

Common verbs that take the **accusative reflexive pronoun** are:

sich interessieren (für)	to be interested (in)
sich treffen (mit)	to meet
sich beschäftigen (mit)	to be busy with
sich konzentrieren (auf)	to concentrate (on)
sich entspannen	to relax
sich entscheiden	to decide

H Common verbs that take the **dative reflexive pronoun** are:

sich wünschen	to wish
sich Sorgen machen (um)	to worry (about)

*Ich mache **mir** Sorgen um meine Zukunft.*
I worry about my future.

Note that only the ***ich*** and ***du*** forms are different in the **dative** case. They become ***mir*** and ***dir***. All the other dative forms are the same as the accusative forms.

H If there is only **one object** in the sentence, the reflexive pronoun will be in the **accusative case**.

*Ich verletze **mich**.* I injure (myself).

If there are **two objects** in the sentence, the reflexive pronoun will be in the dative case.

*Ich verletze mir **das Bein**.* I injure my leg.

Some verbs have a different meaning depending on whether the reflexive pronoun is in the accusative or the dative case, e.g. *sich vorstellen.*

*Ich stelle **mich** vor.* I introduce myself.
*Ich stelle mir **vor**, dass ...* I imagine that ...

H 5 Complete these sentences with the correct form of the reflexive pronoun.

1 Wünscht ihr .... auch ein gutes Gehalt?

2 Ich mache .... keine Sorgen um die Jobsuche, denn ich habe positive Gedanken.

3 Wir möchten .... noch nicht entscheiden, da wir sowieso noch etwas Zeit haben.

4 Sein Vater sorgt .... speziell um ihn, weil seine Chancen in dem Unternehmen nicht sehr hoch sein werden.

5 Du solltest .... mehr konzentrieren, sonst schaffst du die Prüfung nicht.

6 Kannst du .... vorstellen, dass eine gute Ausbildung eine große Bedeutung für mich hat?

F 6 Translate these sentences into German.

1 I am interested in the training at the company

....

2 She is looking forward to the conversation with the teacher.

....

3 They get on well with their colleagues. ....

4 He hopes that he earns a lot of money. ....

5 We meet each other and look for a job on the internet.

....

H 7 Translate these sentences into English on a separate sheet.

1 Wir werden nicht in die Oberstufe gehen.

2 Nach ihren Prüfungen wird sie sich erst entspannen.

3 Du interessierst dich sehr für Autos und wirst im September eine Lehre machen.

4 Ich wünsche mir auf jeden Fall, dass ich nach meiner Ausbildung einen gut bezahlten Job finde.

5 Ihr möchtet euch auch immer weiterbilden.

2 Was ist dein Traumberuf?

- **F** Using *werden* (to become)
- **F** Forming past participles of *-ieren* verbs

1 Complete each sentence using nouns from the box.

For job nouns, you add ***-in*** to the end of the masculine form to create the feminine one. Some feminine job nouns also take an umlaut.

Arzt Journalistin
Polizistin Ärztin Betreuer

1 Tim und Charlotte möchten als .... und .... arbeiten und kranken Menschen helfen.

2 Alina will als .... bei der Polizei arbeiten: Das ist ihr Traum.

3 Elias hat einen Plan: Er will später als .... mit Jugendlichen arbeiten.

4 Layla hat einen Wunsch: Sie schreibt gern und will als .... bei einer Zeitung arbeiten.

G

The irregular verb **werden** can be used:
- for the future tense: *Ich* ***werde*** *morgen ins Kino gehen.*
- to mean 'to become' (or 'get/turn into something'):

Ich <u>möchte</u> Arzt ***werden****.*	I would like to **become** a doctor.
Das Essen ***wird*** *<u>kalt</u>.*	The food **is getting** cold.
Die Kinder ***werden*** *<u>müde</u>.*	The children **are getting/becoming** tired.

ich werde
du wirst
er/sie/es/man wird
wir werden
ihr werdet
Sie/sie werden

2 Circle the correct form of *werden* to complete each sentence.

1 Mein Bruder will Polizist **wird** / **werden**: Das ist sein Ziel.

2 Sie **wird** / **werden** Verkäuferin von Beruf.

3 Er **werden** / **wird** sich viele Informationen über den Beruf holen.

4 Willst du träumen, kreativ sein und Künstler **werdet** / **werden**?

H 5 Mein Geld ist knapp, also will ich einfach nur viel Geld haben und reich **werde** / **werden**!

3 Complete these sentences with the past participle of the verb in brackets.

G For the past participle of ***-ieren*** verbs you don't add *ge-*:

infinitive	**past participle**
akzeptieren	akzeptier**t**
organisieren	organisier**t**
passieren	passier**t**
studieren	studier**t**

1 Wie ist dieser Fehler ....? (*passieren*)

2 Ich habe mich schon immer für einen Job als Polizist .... (*interessieren*)

3 Ich bin in den Sommerferien nach Deutschland .... (*fahren*)

4 Wir wollten durch unsere Arbeit tausend Kunden erreichen, aber es hat nicht .... (*funktionieren*)

5 Aus diesem Grund haben die 16-jährigen Schüler mit ihrem Lehrer .... (*diskutieren*)

4 Translate these sentences into German on a separate sheet.

1 She would like to become a German teacher.

2 We are getting ill.

3 My parents both studied and worked as doctors.

4 He wants to have his own company.

5 My parents have not accepted that.

2 Was ist dein Traumberuf?

- **H** Using *werden* in different tenses
- **H** Revising the conditional and imperfect subjunctive

Module 8
Student Book pp. 184–85

H 1 Complete each sentence using a noun from the box.

Wissenschaftler   Traumberuf
Bühne   Industrie

1 Ich habe den Wunsch, mit meinem Freund eine Firma in der Kaffee-.................................... zu gründen.

2 Wir möchten nicht im Büro arbeiten, stattdessen wollen wir gern .... werden.

3 Ich möchte gern Schauspielerin werden und auf einer .... stehen.

4 Ich muss noch über meinen .... nachdenken.

G

H The **conditional** is formed using ***würde*** + infinitive. *Würde* means 'would'.
*Ich **würde** zum Vorstellungsgespräch gehen.* I **would** go to the job interview.
Use it with ***gern*** to say what you would like to do.
*Ich **würde gern** ein freiwilliges Jahr machen.* I **would like** to do a voluntary year.

sein, ***haben***, ***sollen*** and ***mögen*** are usually used in the **imperfect subjunctive** to express a conditional idea:
*Ein gutes Gehalt **wäre** eine Bedingung.* A good salary **would be** a condition.
*Ich **hätte** viel Erfolg als Anwalt.* I **would have** a lot of success as a lawyer.
*Sie **sollte** Bäuerin werden.* She **should** / **ought to** become a farmer.
*Er **möchte** später Bauer werden.* He **would like** to become a farmer.

H 2 Circle the correct form of the conditional to complete each sentence.

1 Ich **würde** / **wäre** / **hätte** gegen die Arbeitslosigkeit kämpfen.

2 Vor allem **würde** / **wäre** / **hätte** ich gern mehrere Herausforderungen.

3 **Würdest** / **Wärst** / **Hättest** du gern dein Abitur machen oder lieber in einer Fabrik arbeiten?

4 Was **würden** / **wären** / **hätten** die Arbeitnehmer dazu sagen?

5 Anwältin zu werden, **würde** / **wäre** / **hätte** mein absoluter Traum!

If there is an infinitive at the end of the sentence, you will need to use a form of *würd-*.

H 3 Complete these sentences with the correct form of *werden*.

1 Meine Geschwister sind vor zwei Jahren beide Polizisten ....

2 Die Situation auf dem Arbeitsmarkt .... jedes Jahr schwieriger.

3 Ihr Traum, ein Unternehmen zu gründen, ... letztes Jahr Wirklichkeit.

4 Jedes Jahr .... die Möglichkeiten, einen guten Job zu finden, immer geringer.

5 Leider .... wir keine andere Wahl haben.

G

Read the grammar box on the previous page. ***Werden*** can also be used in past tenses.
Imperfect tense: *Das Essen **wurde** kalt.* The food **got** cold.
Perfect tense: *Das Essen **ist** kalt **geworden**.* The food **has got** cold.

H 4 Translate these sentences into German on a separate sheet.

1 It is my wish to become a teacher.

2 As a doctor, my goal would be to help people.

3 If he avoids mistakes, he will be successful.

4 She would start a company if she had enough money.

5 After school he became an actor.

3 Was kannst du gut?

Revising subordinating conjunctions

1 Unjumble the letters to rewrite the words correctly. Then translate them into English.

1 aTme ....

2 quoKeensnz ....

3 eSdnttu ....

H 4 täVdnisersn ....

H 5 iFehkäitg ....

2 Complete these sentences by translating the verbs in brackets into German.

1 Ich bin sehr organisiert und kann gut .... *(to plan)*

2 Ich kann sehr gut .... und habe immer neue Ideen. *(to talk)*

3 Ich kann junge Menschen gut .... *(to understand)*

4 Ich kann den Artikel vom Englischen ins Deutsche .... *(to translate)*

G

Subordinating conjunctions link clauses together and send the verb to the end of the clause.

als when (in the past)	*obwohl* although
da because, since	*bevor* before
dass that	*weil* because
nachdem after	*wenn* if, when

Ich war klein. ⟶ *Ich wollte Ärztin werden,* ***als*** *ich klein war.*

I wanted to become a doctor, **when** I was little.

When you start with the subordinating conjunction, the verbs of both parts meet in the middle, around a comma. This is called a 'verb-comma-verb' structure.

Als *ich klein war, wollte ich Ärztin werden.*

When I was little, I wanted to become a doctor.

H Other examples of **subordinating conjunctions** are:

seitdem since then, since	*ob* whether, if
indem while, by	*solange* as long as
sobald as soon as	

Sobald *ich im Internet gesucht habe, habe ich eine große Anzahl an Jobs gefunden.*

As soon as I searched the internet, I found a large number of jobs.

G

You have already seen verbs in the imperfect tense:

ich ***war*** ...	I **was**
ich ***hatte*** ...	I **had**
es ***gab*** ...	there **was / were**

You can use **modal verbs** with an infinitive in the imperfect tense:

Ich ***wollte*** *in einem Team arbeiten.*

I **wanted** to work in a team.

Ich ***musste*** *studieren.*

I **had** to study.

Ich ***konnte*** *der Umwelt helfen.*

I **could / was able** to help the environment.

Ich ***durfte*** *eine Ausbildung machen.*

I **was allowed** to do a training course.

3 On a separate sheet, rewrite each sentence, putting the words in the subordinate clause into the correct order.

1 Ich wollte Polizistin werden, *war ich jünger als*

2 Sie wollte Tierärztin werden, *liebt sie weil Pferde*

3 Ich werde im Umweltschutz arbeiten, *mein gemacht ich Studium habe nachdem*

4 Er sagt, *dass hat er gute viele Ideen*

5 Ich weiß jedoch noch nicht, *Universität welche ich auf gehe*

H 6 Ich konnte mich leider nicht verbessern, *ich viel obwohl habe gelernt*

Remember that the subordinating conjunction comes after the comma and that it sends the verb to the end of the clause.

4 Rewrite each sentence, starting with the subordinate clause.

Remember the 'verb-comma-verb' structure.

1 Sie will Künstlerin werden, wenn sie 20 Jahre alt ist.

....

2 Ich habe mich verbessert, als die Lehrer gut waren.

....

3 Es ist nicht möglich, dass er jetzt arbeitslos ist.

....

H 4 Ich habe viel Verständnis für andere Menschen, obwohl ich noch ziemlich jung bin.

....

H 5 Ich möchte später Lehrer werden, weil ich gut erklären kann.

....

H 6 Ich bin mir noch nicht sicher, ob ich einen guten Abschluss haben werde.

....

H **5 On a separate sheet, rewrite each pair of sentences as one sentence, starting with the subordinating conjunction in brackets.**

1 Ich lerne nicht mehr so viel. Meine Noten sind schlechter geworden. (*seitdem*)

Seitdem ich nicht mehr so viel lerne, sind meine Noten schlechter geworden.

2 Die Prüfungen sind vorbei. Ihr werdet um die Welt reisen. (*sobald*)

3 Sie hat für den Naturschutz gearbeitet. Sie hat viel für die Umwelt getan. (*indem*)

4 Mein Studium war vorbei. Ich habe ich mir eine Stelle als Arzt gesucht. (*nachdem*)

5 Wir sind auf die Universität gegangen. Wir hatten bereits einen Job in dem Unternehmen. (*bevor*)

6 Ich sehe den Fehler. Ich habe keine Erklärung dafür. (*obwohl*)

H **6 Translate these sentences into English on a separate sheet.**

1 Ich bin gut mit Sprachen.

2 Sie sagt, dass sie immer viele gute Ideen hat.

3 Als ich jünger war, war ich sehr geduldig.

4 Obwohl ich Tiere liebe, durfte ich als Kind nie ein Pferd haben.

5 Wenn ich mehr Geld habe, werde ich in die schöne Schweiz reisen.

H **7 Translate these sentences into German on a separate sheet.**

1 When I was little, I always wanted to stand on a big stage.

2 As soon as I was old enough, I looked for a job.

3 Before I went to university, I did an apprenticeship.

4 While I was still learning, I was already working with young people.

5 After I had my degree, I worked.

4 Ein Zwischenjahr? Warum nicht?

F Revising relative clauses • F Asking questions

1 Complete each sentence using a word from the box.

Ende   Zukunft   Moment   Jahr   Erfahrungen

In English, we say 'gain experience', but in German, we say 'win' or 'collect/gather' experience(s).

1 Ich möchte ein freiwilliges .... im Ausland machen.

2 Ich möchte in der .... im Umweltschutz arbeiten, weil ich die Natur liebe.

3 Ich möchte viele neue .... gewinnen.

4 Was will ich nach der Schule machen? Im .... weiß ich noch nicht.

5 Am .... möchte ich in einem fremden Land leben.

Remember that **relative pronouns** (*der, die, das, die* – who, which, that) refer back to someone or something. They send the verb to the end of the clause, and they always come after a comma in German.
*ein Job, **der** mir Spaß macht* a job **which** is fun

Remember that there are two ways to form a question in German.
- Invert the **verb** and the subject of the sentence: ***Warst** du im Ausland?*
- Use a **question word**: ***Wo** warst du?*

2 Complete these sentences with the correct relative pronoun.

1 Ich möchte in meinem freiwilligen Jahr ein Land besuchen, ... ich noch nicht kenne.

2 Er ist ein Mensch, ... gern mit Kindern arbeitet.

3 Ich möchte Kulturen kennenlernen, ... mir bis jetzt noch fremd sind.

4 Ich kann gut Englisch und sogar ein bisschen Deutsch, aber ich will eine Sprache lernen, ... ich noch nicht kann.

5 Ich will keinen Job, ... hart ist, denn ich will glücklich sein.

3 On a separate sheet, rewrite each sentence, putting the words in the question into the correct order.

genommen and *gestanden* are the past participles of *nehmen* and *stehen*.

1 freiwilliges willst dein machen Wo du Jahr?

2 du als genommen Schüler einen Job Hast?

3 Sie gestanden vielen einmal schon vor Haben Menschen?

4 bedeutet Ausbildung Was eine für dich gute?

5 machst Jahr du im Job Welchen freiwilligen?

4 Translate these sentences into German on a separate sheet.

1 Next year I'm doing a voluntary year.

2 I want to help people who are ill.

3 He has a job that is very interesting.

4 I am very interested in other cultures.

5 In the end, my year abroad was a very positive experience.

4 Ein Zwischenjahr? Warum nicht?

H Using adjectives as nouns

H 1 Complete these sentences by translating the words in brackets into German.

1 Mein freiwilliges Jahr ist sehr .... und hat mir bisher sehr gutgetan. (*interesting*)

2 Es ist nicht ...., einen Job mit einem guten Lohn zu finden. (*easy*)

3 Auch die Reichen sollten mal eine .... Erfahrung machen. (*other*)

4 Meine Kollegen vom Umweltschutz behandeln mich gut und sind sehr .... (*nice, kind*)

5 Ich erwarte sehr .... Gutes von meinem freiwilligen Jahr. (*a lot of*)

G

H Adjectives can be used as a **noun** after *etwas* (something), *nichts* (nothing), *viel* (a lot), *wenig* (little), and *alles* (everything). Just add a capital letter to the adjective and an ending.

- After *etwas, nichts, viel, wenig*, add **-es**:

Etwas Nettes *ist passiert.*
Something nice happened.
Es lag ***nichts Neues*** *auf dem Tisch.* There was nothing new (lying) on the table.
Er hat ***viel Gutes*** *getan.* He did a lot of good.

- After *alles*, add **-e**.

Alles Gute *zum Geburtstag!*
All the best on your birthday!

- You can also use the **comparative form** of the adjective together with *als*:

Es gibt ***nichts Besseres*** *als ...*
There is **nothing better** than ...
Es gibt ***viel Interessanteres*** *als ...* There are many **more interesting** things than ...

H 2 Circle the correct adjectival noun to complete each sentence.

1 Ich möchte ihm etwas **Nützliches / Nützliche** für sein freiwilliges Jahr schenken.

2 Es gibt nichts **Schwierigeres / Schwieriger**, als sich für einen Beruf zu entscheiden.

3 Es ist eine Tatsache, dass er in seinem freiwilligen Jahr viel **Interessantes / Interessante** gelernt hat.

4 Er besitzt viele technische Kenntnisse und an seiner Rede kann ich nur wenig **Schlechtes / Schlechte** finden.

5 Zum Glück ist nichts **Schlimmes / Schlimme** passiert!

H 3 Complete these sentences by translating the words in brackets into German.

1 Ich möchte in meinem freiwilligen Jahr künftig .... (*something easy*) machen.

2 Mein freiwilliges Jahr war teilweise langweilig und ich habe .... (*little new*) gelernt.

3 Ich kann mir .... (*nothing more beautiful*) vorstellen als nach meinem Abschluss zu reisen.

4 Im freiwilligen Jahr kann man .... (*much useful*) tun.

5 Es hat mir große Freude gemacht, ... (*everything foreign*) kennenzulernen.

H 4 Translate these sentences into German on a separate sheet.

1 She did a lot of good.

2 All the best for your journey!

3 I see little of interest here.

4 I would like to do something useful for a few months.

5 There's nothing worse than having no future.

5 Meine Träume für die Zukunft

- Dealing with unfamiliar vocabulary
- Using *hoffen auf* and *hoffen, dass*

1 Draw lines to match up the German words with their English translations.

1 die Rolle	**a** colleague
2 der Chef	**b** partner
3 die Kollegin	**c** support
4 der Partner	**d** workplace
5 die Unterstützung	**e** role
6 der Arbeitsplatz	**f** present
H 7 die Gegenwart	**g** boss

2 Complete each sentence using a verb from the box.

wollen vorbereiten tun heiraten geben werden bringen

1 In der Zukunft wird es viele interessante Jobs ....

2 Was wird die Zukunft ....?

3 Wir hoffen, dass wir nette Partner finden und später vielleicht auch ....

4 Wir müssen uns alle auf unsere Zukunft gut ....

H 5 In der Zukunft .... vielleicht Computer, die allein fahren, das Essen zu uns nach Hause liefern.

H 6 Meine Eltern ...., dass ich studiere. Aber können sie mich dazu zwingen?

H 7 Ich muss noch überlegen, was ich künftig .... möchte.

G

The verb ***hoffen*** can be used in different ways:

- *Ich* ***hoffe auf*** + accusative noun (I'm **hoping for** ...)

Ich ***hoffe auf*** *einen interessanten Job.*

- *Ich* ***hoffe, dass*** ... (I'm **hoping that** ...)

Remember that *dass* sends the verb to the end of the clause.

Ich ***hoffe, dass*** *die Arbeit interessant ist.*

Ich ***hoffe, dass*** *ich eine interessante Arbeit finde.*

H *Ich* ***hoffe, dass*** *ich eine interessante Arbeit finden werde.*

G

There are a number of ways to work out the meaning of words you have not seen before:

- Look for **cognates** and **near-cognates** (words that look very similar to English words): e.g. *rund* (round), **H** *Faktor* – factor. But be careful of 'false friends': e.g. *Chef* (boss, not chef), *bald* (soon, not bald).
- Break **compound nouns** down: *Zahnarzt* – *Zahn* + *Arzt* (tooth + doctor – dentist); **H** *Haushalt* – *Haus* + *halten* (house + hold – household, budget).
- Use the **context** to work out the meaning.
- Use **word families**: e.g. **H** *prüfen* (to test, examine) – *die Prüfung* (exam, test); **H** *zählen* (to count) – *die Zahl* (number); **H** *künstlich* (artificial) – *die Kunst* (art).

3 Complete these sentences by translating the phrases in brackets into German. Use the correct form of *hoffen* and *auf* + noun or *dass* + clause.

1 Ich hoffe auf .... (*a wonderful partner*).

2 Er hofft, dass .... (*he passes the exam*).

3 Wir hoffen auf .... (*a job abroad*).

4 Sie hofft, dass .... (*she studies science*).

5 Ihr hofft auf .... (*an exciting voluntary year*).

4 Rewrite each sentence, using *hoffen* + *auf/dass* as indicated.

> In subordinate clauses that follow *dass*, you need a subject and a verb, and the verb goes to the end of the clause. You will need to think of a verb that will make sense in the context (e.g. *haben* or *bekommen*).

1 Wir hoffen auf eine glückliche Zukunft.

Wir hoffen, dass ....

2 Sie hofft, dass sie viele gute Chancen im Leben hat.

Sie hofft auf ....

3 Ich hoffe auf einen freundlichen Chef und nette Kollegen in meiner Ausbildung.

Ich hoffe, dass ....

4 Die Mehrheit der Schüler hofft, dass sie einen Job im Umweltschutz finden wird.

Die Mehrheit der Schüler hofft auf ....

H 5 Er hat noch Zweifel, aber er hofft trotzdem auf gute Noten und einen guten Abschluss.

Er hat noch Zweifel, aber er hofft trotzdem, dass ....

H 5 Complete these German sentences using *ich hoffe auf* and *ich hoffe, dass,* and the ideas in brackets.

1 (*do a successful apprenticeship*)

Ich hoffe auf ....

Ich hoffe, dass ....

2 (*have/get support from my family*)

Ich hoffe auf ....

Ich hoffe, dass ....

3 (*learn many new skills*)

Ich hoffe auf ....

Ich hoffe, dass ....

F 6 Translate these sentences into German on a separate sheet.

1 He would like to work abroad.

2 We want an interesting job and a lot of money.

3 I hope to have a big family.

4 She hopes to have lots of new friends at university.

5 Getting married is not so important to me.

H 7 Translate these sentences into English on a separate sheet.

1 Ich muss mich bald entscheiden, was ich in der Zukunft machen will.

2 Ich habe noch nicht so viel darüber nachgedacht.

3 Ich hoffe, dass ich nach meiner Lehre gleich eine Arbeit finden werde.

4 Ich brauche einen guten Abschluss, um auf die Universität zu gehen.

5 Ich möchte einen Job, der eine Herausforderung für mich ist.

Glossary

bold = this word will appear in Higher exams only

German	English
Abitur (nt)	*school leaving exam, A levels*
Abschluss (m)	*school leaving certificate, degree, diploma*
Alltag (m)	*daily routine, everyday life*
Anwalt (m)	*lawyer (m), solicitor*
Anwältin (f)	*lawyer (f), solicitor*
Anzahl (f)	*number (count, amount), quantity*
Arbeit (f)	*work, job, employment*
arbeiten (an dat. + noun)	*(to) work (on + noun)*
Arbeitgeber (m)	*employer*
Arbeitnehmer (m)	*employee, worker*
arbeitslos	*unemployed*
Arbeitslosigkeit (f)	*unemployment*
Arbeitsplatz (m)	*workplace, job, employment*
Artikel (m)	*article*
Arzt (m)	*doctor (m)*
Ärztin (f)	*doctor (f)*
Ausbildung (f)	*training, education, development*
aussehen	*(to) appear, look*
außerdem	*besides, in addition, furthermore*
Bauer (m)	*farmer (m)*
Bäuerin (f)	*farmer (f)*
bedeuten	*(to) mean*
Bedeutung (f)	*meaning, significance*
Bedingung (f)	*condition, stipulation, requirement*
behandeln	*(to) treat*

German	English
beide	*both, the two*
bereit	*ready*
bereits	*already*
Beruf (m)	*occupation, job, profession*
beschäftigen; sich acc. beschäftigen mit (+ noun)	*(to) employ; (to) be busy, deal with (+ noun)*
besitzen	*(to) own, have*
Betreuer (m)	*carer, care worker (m)*
bevor	*before*
bilden	*(to) educate, form*
bisher	*until now, up to now, yet, so far*
bringen	*(to) bring*
Bühne (f)	*stage*
Chance (f)	*chance, opportunity*
Chef (m)	*boss*
da (adv)	*there*
da (conj)	*because, since, as, given that*
die Reichen (pl)	*the rich (ones)*
einfach	*simple, easy, simply, easily*
Ende (nt)	*end, finish*
entscheiden; sich acc. entscheiden (für + noun)	*(to) decide; (to) decide (on + noun)*
Entscheidung (f)	*decision*
Erfahrung (f)	*experience*
erfolgreich	*successful*
erklären; sich acc. erklären	*(to) explain; (to) declare oneself*
Erklärung (f)	*explanation*
erwarten	*(to) expect*
etwas (Nettes)	*something (nice)*
Euro (m)	*euro*

Fabrik (f)	*factory*
Fähigkeit (f)	*ability, capability, skill*
Faktor (m)	*factor*
Fall (m)	*fall, case*
Fehler (m)	*mistake, error*
Firma (f)	*firm, company, business*
Firmen (pl)	*firms, companies, businesses*
freiwillig	*voluntary, voluntarily*
fremd	*foreign, strange*
geben	*(to) give*
(aux) ... gedacht	*thought / (have, has) thought (pp)*
Gedanke (m)	*thought, idea*
Gegenwart (f)	*present*
Gehalt (nt)	*salary, pay, earnings, wages*
Geld (nt)	*money, cash*
Gelegenheit (f)	*opportunity, chance*
(aux) ... genommen	*took, had something to eat or drink / (have, has) taken (pp), had something to eat or drink*
gering	*low, small*
Gesellschaft (f)	*society, company*
Gespräch (nt)	*conversation, talk*
(aux) ... gestanden	*stood / (have, has) stood (pp)*
(aux) ... getan	*did, put / (have, has) done, put (pp)*
gewinnen	*(to) win / winning*
gleich	*same, right away, just, immediately, straight away, equal*
glücklich	*happy, fortunate, happily*
Grund (m)	*reason, basis*
gründen	*(to) establish, found*
hart	*hard*
Haushalt (m)	*household, budget*
heiraten	*(to) marry*
heraus	*out, outside*
Herausforderung (f)	*challenge*
Hilfe (f)	*help, assistance*
hoffen (auf acc. + noun)	*(to) hope (for + noun)*
hoffentlich	*hopefully*
holen	*(to) get, fetch*
Idee (f)	*idea*
indem	*while, by*
Industrie (f)	*industry*
-jährig	*years old*
jedoch	*however*
Job (m)	*job*
Journalist (m)	*journalist (m)*
Kenntnis (f)	*knowledge*
knapp	*scarce, slim*
Kollege (m)	*colleague (m), co-worker (m)*
Kollegin (f)	*colleague (f), co-worker (f)*
Konsequenz (f)	*consequence*
krank	*sick, ill*
kreativ	*creative(ly)*
Kunde (m)	*customer (m), client (m)*
Kundin (f)	*customer (f), client (f)*
künftig	*future, from now on*

künstlich	*artificial(ly)*			
lag	*(I, she, he, it) lay, was situated*			
langfristig	*long-term, in the long run*			
legen; sich legen	*(to) lay, put; (to) lie down*			
Lehre (f)	*apprenticeship*			
leisten; sich dat. leisten	*(to) perform, achieve, do; (to) afford*			
liefern	*(to) deliver, supply*			
Lohn (m)	*wage, pay, salary*			
Lust (f)	*desire*			
Lust (auf + noun) haben	*(to) feel like (+ noun)*			
mehrere	*several, multiple, various*			
Mehrheit (f)	*majority*			
möglich	*possible*			
Möglichkeit (f)	*possibility, chance, opportunity*			
Moment (m)	*moment, instant*			
nachdem	*after*			
nachdenken	*(to) think about, reflect*			
neu	*new, recent*			
noch	*still, yet, else*			
ob	*whether, if*			
Oberstufe (f)	*sixth form*			
obwohl	*although*			
ohne	*without*			
ohne ... zu (+ infinitive)	*without (+ verb)*			
Partner (m)	*partner (m)*			
Pferd (nt)	*horse*			
pflegen	*(to) care, cultivate, nurse*			
Plan (m)	*plan*			
planen	*(to) plan, design*			
Polizei (f)	*police*			
Polizist (m)	*police officer (m)*			
Prozent (nt)	*percent*			
prüfen	*(to) examine, check*			
Rede (f)	*speech, talk*			
reden	*(to) talk | talking*			
reich	*rich, wealthy, abundant*			
Rolle (f)	*role, part*			
rund	*round*			
sagen	*(to) say, tell*			
Satz (m)	*sentence, phrase*			
schenken	*(to) give (as a present)*			
schon	*already, yet*			
schön	*lovely, beautiful*			
Schutz (m)	*protection, conservation*			
seitdem	*since (then)*			
selbst, selber	*self, even*			
sich	*himself, herself, itself, oneself, yourself (formal), themselves, yourselves (formal) (reflex) / each other (recip)*			
sicher	*safe, secure, certain, sure, of course*			
sitzen bleiben, sitzenbleiben	*(to) repeat a school year*			
sobald	*as soon as*			
sogar	*even, in fact, actually*			
sogenannt	*so-called*			
solange	*as long as*			
sonst	*otherwise, else*			
sowieso	*anyway*			
speziell	*special, specific*			

German	English
statt	*instead of*
statt ... zu (+ infinitive)	*instead of (+ verb)*
stattdessen	*instead*
stehen	*(to) stand*
Stelle (f)	*place, job, position*
Student (m)	*student (m)*
studieren	*(to) study (at university)*
Studium (nt)	*study, studies*
Suche (f)	*search*
suchen	*(to) search for, look for*
Tatsache (f)	*fact*
Team (nt)	*team*
technisch	*technical*
teilweise	*partly, partially*
Traum (m)	*dream*
träumen	*(to) dream*
tun	*(to) do, put*
überlegen	*(to) consider, think about, think of*
übersetzen	*(to) translate*
unbedingt	*absolutely*
Universität, Uni (f)	*university, uni*
unterhalten; sich acc. unterhalten	*(to) entertain; (to) amuse oneself, chat*
Unternehmen (nt)	*company, firm*
Unterstützung (f)	*support*
verdienen	*(to) earn, deserve*
Verkäufer (m)	*shop assistant, sales person (m)*
verschieden	*different, various, diverse*
Verständnis (nt)	*understanding, sympathy*
verstehen; sich verstehen (mit)	*(to) understand; (to) get on well with*
vorbereiten (auf acc. + noun)	*(to) prepare (for + noun)*
vorhaben	*(to) have in mind, be planning, intend*
vorstellen; sich dat. vorstellen	*(to) introduce; (to) imagine*
Vorstellung (f)	*idea, introduction, performance, imagination*
Vorstellungsgespräch (nt)	*job interview*
Wahl (f)	*choice, election, selection*
wahrscheinlich	*likely, probable / probably*
weiß	*(I) know (something) / (she, he, it, one) knows (something)*
weiter	*further, (carry) on*
weitere (r, s)	*additional, further, another*
wert	*worth, worthy of*
wiederholen	*(to) repeat*
Wissenschaftler (m)	*scientist (m)*
Wunsch (m)	*wish, desire*
wünschen	*(to) want, wish, desire*
zählen	*(to) count*
Ziel (nt)	*destination, goal, aim, target*
Zweifel (m)	*doubt*
zwingen	*(to) force, compel*

Foundation translation revision

German to English

1 Rewrite each English translation, putting the words into the correct order.

1 Ich möchte Künstler werden. — *artist become I like an would to*

....

2 Ich habe meinen Laptop vergessen. — *forgotten I laptop have my*

....

3 Wir haben in den Ferien in einer Wohnung gewohnt. — *stayed holidays in we In a flat the*

....

wohnen can mean 'to live' or, when talking about holidays, 'to stay'. When translating, use the one that works best in the context of the sentence.

4 Ich interessiere mich für die Berge und die Küste. — *interested in coast mountains am and the I the*

....

5 Alle Menschen sollen die Umwelt schützen. — *environment protect Everybody should the*

....

2 Draw lines to match up the German sentences with their English translations.

1 Ich möchte Polizistin werden.

2 Die Ärztin hat ihre Tasche vergessen.

3 Wir haben in einem Hotel geschlafen.

4 Ich interessiere mich für fremde Kulturen.

5 Alle Menschen sollen Glas recyceln.

a Everybody should recycle glass.

b I am interested in foreign cultures.

c The doctor forgot her bag.

d We slept in a hotel.

e I would like to become a police officer.

3 Underline the mistake(s) in the English translations and write out the translations correctly on a separate sheet.

1 Ich möchte Lehrer werden. — *I would like to be a teacher.*

2 Ich habe mein Ticket verloren. — *I have lost my money.*

3 Wir haben an der Küste gewohnt. — *We stayed in the mountains.*

4 Ich interessiere mich sehr für Tiere. — *I am very interested in the weather.*

5 Man soll Papier sammeln. — *We should recycle paper.*

4 Translate these sentences into English on a separate sheet.

1 Ich möchte Ärztin werden.

2 Ich interessiere mich sehr für die Umwelt.

3 Wir sollen Glas sammeln und recyceln.

4 Ich habe meine Tasche verloren.

5 Wir haben letztes Wochenende in einem Hotel auf einem Berg gewohnt.

English to German

1 Colour one box from each column to translate each sentence into German. Use a different colour for each sentence. Then write out your translations.

Ich werde	auf eine	in Berlin	gegangen.
Wir sind	im Team	Geld	sehr wichtig.
Ich warte	viel	ist für mich	im Geschäft.
Die Arbeit	durfte	ins Museum	haben.
Ich	gestern	freie Stelle	studieren.

1 I will have a lot of money. ....

2 We went to the museum yesterday. ....

3 I am waiting for a free position in the shop. ....

4 Working in a team is very important to me. ....

5 I was allowed to study in Berlin. ....

2 Complete each translation into German using a word from the box.

Stelle Schloss
Besuch Ferien Team

1 On Monday I will organise my holidays. *Am Montag werde ich meine .... organisieren.*

2 We worked very well in a team. *Wir haben sehr gut in einem .... gearbeitet.*

3 I am looking forward to my visit to the company. *Ich freue mich auf meinen .... in der Firma.*

4 A position at the university is quite important to me. *Eine .... an der Universität ist mir ziemlich wichtig.*

5 I was allowed to visit the castle on the island. *Ich durfte das .... auf der Insel besuchen.*

3 Complete these sentences by translating the words in brackets into German.

1 Ich .... (*will*) in einem Team .... (*work*).

2 Er hat .... (*the university*) .... (*visited*).

3 Ich .... (*am looking forward to*) unsere Ferien .... (*in the hotel*).

4 Ein guter Job ist .... (*very important to me*).

5 Ich .... (*was allowed*) im Museum nicht laut .... (*speak*).

4 Translate these sentences into German.

1 I will visit the beautiful museum. ....

2 We organised our holidays on an island. ....

3 I am looking forward to working in a team. ....

4 A lot of money is very important to me. ....

5 She was allowed to go to university. ....

Higher translation revision

German to English

1 Circle the odd one out.

1 Unternehmen / Ausflug / Vorstellungsgespräch / Wirtschaft

2 Abitur / Oberstufe / Umwelt / Abschluss

3 bereit / wünschen / kämpfen / reisen

4 hätte / welche / würde / wäre

5 nützlich / toll / gründen / verschieden

6 nachdem / sobald / seitdem / danach

2 Complete these sentences by translating the words in brackets into English.

1 After I .... (*habe studiert*) commerce, ... (*werde ich*) .... (*gründen*) my own company.

2 .... (*Ich wünsche mir*) a job with a lot of .... (*Verantwortung*).

3 I would like to do .... (*etwas Nützliches für die Gesellschaft*) and to fight against .... (*Klimawandel*).

4 I am ready .... (*ein freiwilliges Jahr zu machen*).

5 .... (*Welches Unternehmen*) will you choose?

3 Correct the English translations by crossing through the incorrect word(s) and writing the correction above or next to it.

1 Sobald ich meinen Abschluss gemacht habe, werde ich ins Ausland reisen.
After I have done my school leaving certificate, I will work abroad.

2 Ich möchte unbedingt fremde Länder sehen und was Tolles erleben.
I absolutely want to see foreign countries and experience something useful.

3 Ich würde gern um die ganze Welt fliegen, aber das ist zu teuer.
I want to fly around the whole world, but that is too expensive.

4 Und es ist auch nicht gut für die Umwelt und den Klimawandel.
And it is also not good for the progress and climate change.

5 Danach bin ich bereit, in einem Unternehmen zu arbeiten. Welche Zukunft siehst du für dich?
Before that, I am ready to work in a school. Which responsibilities do you see for yourself?

4 Translate these sentences into English on a separate sheet.

1 Nachdem ich mein Abitur gemacht habe, werde ich Wirtschaft studieren.

2 Ich wünsche mir eine bessere Gesellschaft und will unbedingt etwas Nützliches tun.

3 Sie würde gern in einem Unternehmen arbeiten, das gegen den Klimawandel kämpft.

4 Wir sind bereit, für den Fortschritt zu arbeiten.

5 Welchen Weg wirst du nach deinem Abschluss gehen?

English to German

1 Draw lines to match up the English with the German words.

1 sixth form	**a** der Zustand
2 glasses	**b** die Krise
3 state	**c** die Lösung
4 project	**d** die Oberstufe
5 solution	**e** die Brille
6 crisis	**f** das Projekt

2 Complete each German translation using a word from the box.

lernen bekommen entdeckt würde vergessen

1 I forgot my key.	*Ich habe meinen Schlüssel* ....
2 We discovered an unbelievably great alternative.	*Wir haben eine unglaublich tolle Alternative* ....
3 I would like to get a good salary.	*Ich* .... *gern ein gutes Gehalt bekommen.*
4 I had to learn a lot in sixth form.	*Ich musste in der Oberstufe viel* ....
5 I want to get many challenges.	*Ich möchte viele Herausforderungen* ....

3 Translate the sentences into German, using the first letter of each word to help you.

1 I lost my glasses.

I ___ h ___ m ___ B ___ v ___.

2 The crisis was unbelievably serious.

D ___ K ___ w ___ u ___ e ___.

3 I would like to do my school leaving certificate soon.

I ___ w ___ g ___ b ___ m ___ A ___ m ___.

4 It is not simple to find a solution.

E ___ i ___ n ___ e ___, e ___ L ___ z ___ f ___.

5 Despite the bad state, the electric car worked.

T ___ d ___ s ___ Z ___ h ___ d ___ E ___ f ___.

4 Translate these sentences into German on a separate sheet.

1 I discovered an unbelievably great project.

2 The electric car was in quite a bad state.

3 It is not easy to get a good income.

4 Despite the crisis there is a solution.

5 I would like to go into sixth form and I therefore have to learn for my school leaving certificate.

Translation strategies: German to English

Here are some useful strategies to help you translate from German into English.

Reading for gist

When you are faced with a passage or sentence to translate from German into English, it is really important to read it through to establish the general meaning, even if you know that there are some words you don't recognise or cannot immediately translate.

Word order

German word order can be very different from English. Before translating, read carefully to the end of each sentence or clause to make sure you take all parts of it into account when pinning down the meaning.

Remember that there are three types of word order in German:

Normal word order

1 *Ich esse oft Gemüse.*

This is normal word order, though slightly different from English: we would translate this as 'I often eat vegetables.', rather than 'I eat often vegetables'.

Inverted word order

2 *Ab und zu esse ich Gemüse.*

In this sentence, the subject and verb are inverted after the time phrase at the start. Translating word for word, would give 'Now and again eat I vegetables.' But, in English we would say 'Now and again I eat vegetables.'

Word order with subordinate clauses

3 *Am Wochenende essen wir Gemüse, weil mein Vater kocht.*

The verb is sent to the end of the clause after a subordinating conjunction (*weil*). Look out for the comma in German, here indicating a separation between two clauses: 'At the weekend we eat vegetables because my father cooks.'

Bear in mind the major word order switch that occurs when the sentence starts with a sub-clause: *Wenn mein Vater kocht, essen wir immer Gemüse.* Look out for the 'verb-comma-verb' structure as a clue to this: 'When my father cooks, we always eat vegetables.'

Using familiar language, cognates and context

Use familiar language, cognates and context to decode the meaning of unknown words:

Die Band hat ein Konzert im Stadion gegeben.

You can probably work out the (near-)cognates *Band* (band), *Konzert* (concert) and *Stadion* (stadium). You may know that *gegeben* is the past participle of *geben* (to give), so you understand that the band gave a concert in the stadium.

Gestern sind wir mit der Straßenbahn bis zum Obstgarten gefahren.

In this sentence, you may know *gestern* (yesterday), *mit* (with) and *sind wir gefahren* (we travelled). You may also know *bis* (up to) and *zu* (to).

For *Straßenbahn*, use the context to make an informed guess. It must be some sort of means of transport, as travel is involved. You know that *Straße* is 'street' and *Bahn* is 'railway', so *Straßenbahn* is literally 'street railway': tram.

The same applies to *Obstgarten*. You may know that *Obst* is 'fruit' and *Garten* is 'garden'. So, *Obstgarten* (literally 'fruit garden') is 'orchard'.

Tricky words and false friends

- Look out for relative clauses (see page 45): relative pronouns (such as *der, die, das*) are not translated as 'the', even though they look similar to the definite article:

  *Ich habe einen Bruder, **der** Max heißt.* I have a brother **who** is called Max.

  *Ich mag den Hund, **den** wir im Park sehen.* I like the dog **which** we see in the park.
- Cognates and near-cognates can help you, but watch out for 'false friends': German words which look similar to English, but have totally different meanings.

  bekommen to receive, get (**not** 'to become')

  fast almost, nearly (**not** 'fast')

Grammar

- Use **tense indicators** and your grammatical knowledge to help you translate the <u>tense</u>:

  Present: ***Heute** <u>fahre</u> ich in die Stadt.* **Today** <u>I am going</u> into town.

  Past: ***Letzte Woche** <u>sind</u> wir nach Hamburg <u>gefahren</u>.* **Last week** we <u>went</u> to Hamburg.

  Future: ***Nächsten Samstag** <u>werden</u> wir nach Wien <u>fahren</u>.* **Next Saturday** <u>we will go</u> to Vienna.
- You can translate some tenses in more than one way. Decide which sounds better in the context:

  Present: *Ich **spiele** Tennis.* → I play / am playing tennis.

  Perfect: *Ich **habe** Tennis **gespielt**.* → I played / have played tennis.

  Imperfect: *Ich **spielte** Tennis.* → I played / was playing / used to play tennis.
- Try to spot infinitives at the end of sentences or clauses. Infinitives are likely to occur in future tense sentences or in sentences where there is a modal verb:

  *Ich **werde** ein Instrument **spielen**.* I **will play** an instrument.

  *Wir **möchten** Käse **essen**.* We **would like to eat** cheese.
- Look out for small words that make a difference to the meaning, such as *gern, nicht* and *kein*:

  *Ich gehe **gern** in die Stadt.* I **like** going into town.

  *Ich gehe **nicht** in die Stadt.* I'm **not** going into town.

  *Ich habe **keine** Schwester.* I **don't** have a sister.
- Umlauts can also change meaning: *schon* = already, *sch**ö**n* = beautiful

  Look out for these comparatives (*groß – größer*) and plurals (*Arzt – Ärzte*).
- Split long compound words up into their various parts to work out the meaning:

  Hauptrolle: Haupt (main) + *Rolle* (role) → main role

Translation skills

- Don't always try to translate word for word. You won't always find that one word in German means one word in English, or vice versa. Similarly, singular nouns in German might equate to plural nouns in English, or vice versa:

  *Ich habe meine **Hausaufgaben** gemacht.* I have done my **homework**.
- Don't be afraid to use different words or a different number of words to get a good translation. However, don't stray too far from the meaning or make random guesses.
- It is important to account for every word in a translation, even if some words don't need translating or if you need to add words for the sentence to make sense. For example:

  Montags spielen wir Fußball. **On** Mondays we play football.

  *Ich freue mich auf **die** Schule.* I'm looking forward to school.
- It is a good idea to read your translation back to yourself (out loud if you can) to check that it makes sense and sounds natural in English.

Translation strategies: English to German

Here are some strategies for when you are translating from English into German. You will need to draw on your knowledge of German grammar and vocabulary, just as for any other writing task.

Reading for gist

When you have a passage or sentence to translate into German, read the whole thing through once to get the gist. Then work phrase by phrase. Be systematic, and check as you are writing: verb forms, tenses, word order, adjective endings, singular and plural nouns, prepositions and cases.

Grammar

- Look out for **tense triggers** in the English, to make sure you have identified which tense to use in German:

  Yesterday I went to the supermarket. → past (perfect) tense needed

  Tomorrow I will go to school. → future tense needed

  Think carefully about the German verb forms, check your endings and make sure you have put the infinitive or past participle (if there is one) in the right place. For the perfect tense, check you have used the correct auxiliary verb.
- Look out for verbs that are **reflexive** or **separable** in German because these aren't always obvious from the English. Make sure you put the reflexive pronoun or separable prefix in the right place in the sentence:

  In the mornings I exercise. *Morgens **bewege** ich **mich**.*

  After that I watch TV. *Danach **sehe** ich **fern**.*
- **H** Remember that to say you have been doing something for a certain length of time, you use ***seit*** + the present tense. *Seit* takes the dative, so make sure you put the dative ending onto a plural noun that follows it:

  I **have been learning** German for three years. *Ich **lerne seit** drei Jahre**n** Deutsch.*
- Remember the three key **imperfect** tense forms provide a simple way of expressing the past:

  I **was** ill. *Ich **war** krank.*

  We **had** a lot of homework. *Wir **hatten** viele Hausaufgaben.*

  There was nothing to eat. ***Es gab** nichts zu essen.*
- You may have to use **modal verbs**, so look out for 'can', 'must', 'should', 'want' and 'allowed to', and remember to send the infinitive to the end of the clause:

  I'm not **allowed** to go to the cinema today. *Ich **darf** heute nicht ins Kino gehen.*

  Look out also for 'could', 'had to', 'was allowed to' and 'wanted', which mean you need to use modal verbs in the imperfect tense:

  As a child, I **wanted** to become a police officer. *Als Kind **wollte** ich Polizist werden.*
- Watch out for 'would' in English. This indicates that you need to use the **conditional** in German, often in the form of *ich möchte*:

  I **would like** to travel. *Ich **möchte** reisen. /* **H** *Ich **würde gern** reisen.*

  H or as *ich würde* + infinitive:

  I **would** never **go** hiking. *Ich **würde** nie wandern **gehen**.*

Time phrases and useful little words

- Learn time and frequency phrases: last week (*letzte Woche*), next weekend (*nächstes Wochenende*), sometimes (*manchmal*), normally (*normalerweise*), etc.
- Build up a bank of intensifiers such as *wirklich, echt, ziemlich*, etc.

Endings

- Learn the case endings for articles, possessive adjectives, adjectives and pronouns. Think systematically about which case is required: look for prepositions that trigger certain cases, check subjects and objects. And don't forget to use a capital letter for all nouns!

Word order

Remember that there are three types of word order in German (see page 148). Think carefully about which one to use for each sentence of your translation. Two key rules are:

1 Verb second

Even if there is a time or place expression at the beginning of the sentence, or even an entire subordinate clause, the **verb** always comes second:

I eat vegetables now and again. *Ab und zu **esse** ich Gemüse.*

In the sentence above, the subject and **verb** have swapped round because the time expression has come first in the sentence.

When my father cooks, we eat vegetables. *Wenn mein Vater kocht, **essen** wir Gemüse.*

Here, a whole subordinate clause is the first 'idea' of the sentence but the main verb (*essen*) still comes second, after the subordinate clause. Remember to use the 'verb-comma-verb' pattern in this kind of construction.

2 Time – Manner – Place

- Always check that you have included the elements of a sentence in the correct order:

  'I eat with my family at home in the evenings.'

  Time: *abends* — Manner: *mit meiner Familie* — Place: *zu Hause*

  Ich esse abends mit meiner Familie zu Hause.

- Remember to send the verb to the end of the clause after a subordinating conjunction such as *weil*. You must always add a comma before *weil* to indicate the start of the subordinate clause:

  We eat meat at the weekend because my sister cooks.

  *Am Wochenende essen wir Fleisch, **weil** meine Schwester **kocht**.*

Translation skills

- Be careful with words that can be missed out in English but must be included in German, and vice versa. These can often be learned as set phrases:

We have a dog called Max.	*Wir haben einen Hund, **der** Max heißt.*
I go **to** school.	*Ich gehe **in die** Schule.*
On Mondays I have German.	***Montags** habe ich Deutsch.*
I would like to be **a teacher**.	*Ich möchte **Lehrer/Lehrerin** werden.*

- Avoid translating word for word when you translate into German. The present and imperfect tenses are expressed in several ways in English, but just one form is used in German:

  Present: I go / am going to the cinema. → *Ich gehe ins Kino.*

  Notice that there are no words for 'am', 'was' or 'used to' in the German translations.

  H Imperfect: I went / was going / used to go to the cinema. → *Ich ging ins Kino.*

- If you don't know how to say something in German, don't worry too much! Try to think of a synonym (a similar word), or another way to say it using vocabulary that you do know.
- There's a lot to think about when translating into German, but don't panic! Work carefully through each sentence and check your spelling, word order and endings thoroughly to be sure that you have written correct German.

Avoid using translation software, lots of which is available online. Although online dictionaries can be helpful for translating individual words, there is no guarantee that any online service will provide you with a correct answer in any context.

Vocabulary learning strategies

In the examination you will be tested on your knowledge of German vocabulary, so learning the vocabulary is really important. But how do you make it stick?

1 Look, cover, write, check: Write out a list of German words with their English translations. Cover one list and write out the translations. Uncover the list and check. What did you get right and what did you get wrong?

2 Create your own flashcards: Write out cards with the German on one side and the English on the other. Remember to write *der*, *die* or *das* with nouns so that you learn their gender. Test yourself with the cards until you've learned them all.

3 Record on a device: Record yourself saying the words for one unit in both languages. Listen back and record yourself again, focusing on the words you're finding it difficult to remember.

4 Get someone else to test you: Give your partner a list of the words you're learning and ask them to call out words for you to translate. It's helpful to test someone else too, so you also see the words.

5 Place sticky notes around the room: Write vocabulary on sticky notes and stick them around the room or on a wall that you often pass. As you pass the note, learn the word. Replace the notes with new ones as you learn.

6 Blurt it out and write it down: Read through the Student Book vocabulary list for a unit. Close the book and say the words/phrases out loud, and then write them down. Check back and write down words you didn't know in a different colour.

Use these strategies to help you organise vocabulary and work out meanings of words.

1 Synonyms and antonyms: Learn pairs of similar words (synonyms) or opposites (antonyms).

schwer (*difficult*)	billig (*cheap*)
schwierig (*difficult*)	teuer (*expensive*)

2 Cognates and false friends: Some words (cognates) mean the same in German and English:

der Sport *sport, PE ...*

Beware of false friends! They look like English words but mean something different:

der Chef *boss ...*

3 Prefixes and suffixes: These can help you work out meanings and even create new words:

Prefix: Haupt- *main* → die Hauptstraße (*main street*)
Suffix: -er: besuchen (*to visit*) → der Besuch**er** (*visitor*)

4 Word families: Create mind maps for word families.

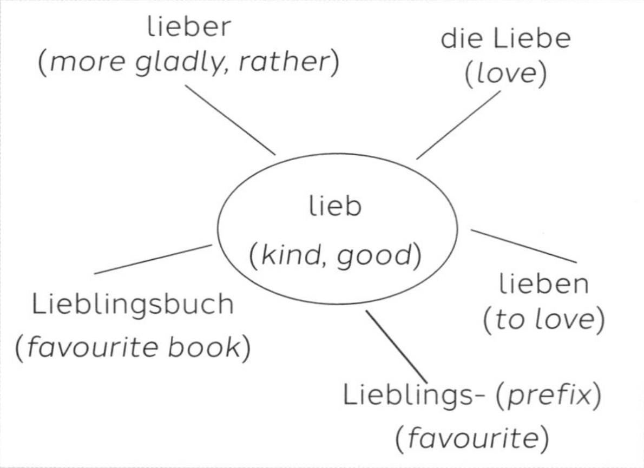

5 Working out genders: Learn patterns for different genders of nouns.
For example:

- all words ending in *-ung*, *-heit* or *-keit* are feminine
- all words ending in *-chen* are neuter.

6 Compound words: Break these down into their component parts:

das Kleidungsgeschäft → Kleidung *clothes* + Geschäft *shop* → *clothes shop*

A compound noun always takes the gender of the last noun.